Caricature Carving from Head to Toe

By Dave Stetson
Photography by Roger Schroeder

Fox Chapel
PUBLISHING

© 2003 by Fox Chapel Publishing Company, Inc.
Caricature Carving from Head to Toe is an original work, first published in 2003 by Fox Chapel Publishing Company, Inc. The patterns contained herein are copyrighted by the author. Artists may make up to three photocopies of each individual pattern for personal use. The patterns, themselves, however, are not to be duplicated for resale or distribution under any circumstances. This is a violation of copyright law.

Step-by-Step Photography   Roger Schroeder

ISBN: 978-1-56523-121-4
Publisher's Cataloging-in-Publication Data

Stetson,Dave.

    Caricature carving from head to toe / by Dave Stetson ; photography
    by Roger Schroeder. -- 1st ed. -- East Petersburg, PA : Fox Chapel
    Pub. Co., c2003.

        p.;cm.

    ISBN:978-1-56523-121-4 ; 1-56523-121-X

        1.Wood-carved figurines--Caricatures and cartoons. 2. Wood-
    carving--Patterns. 3. Caricature .I. Schroeder, Roger, 1945-
    II.Title.

TT199.7 .S754 2003   2003107299
736/.4--dc22   2008

Note to Authors: We are always looking for talented authors to write new books in our area of woodworking, design, and related crafts. Please contact Acquisition Editor, with a brief letter describing your idea at 1970 Broad Street, East Petersburg, PA 17520.

To learn more about the other great books from Fox Chapel Publishing, or to find a retailer near you, call toll-free 800-457-9112 or visit us at *www.FoxChapelPublishing.com*.

Printed in Indonesia

First printing: 2003
Second printing: 2004
Third printing: 2008
Fourth printing: 2011

Table of
Contents

About the Author

Dave Stetson briefly took up carving in 1956 when his grandfather gave him a pocketknife for his tenth birthday. He attempted a relief carving on the top of his elementary school desk, but having to spend every day for two weeks outside the principal's office after school learning the fine art of sanding and refinishing, promptly ended Dave's relief carving career.

Luckily he reignited his passion for woodcarving again in 1984 in the form of caricature. A student of art all his life, Dave is a keen observer of his surroundings. He is able to notice the obscure gesture, the fine detail and the absurd in his fellow man and thus depicts them in his carvings.

A co-creator and founding member of the Caricature Carvers of America, Dave is passionate about his love of caricature and spends countless hours during carving seminars, woodcarving shows and gallery showings expressing his belief that *good* caricature is an exaggeration of realism. Dave is often heard saying, "Caricature is not a realistic carving gone bad!"

Born in 1946 in Pittsburg, California, and moving to Vermont at the tender age of 3 months, Dave spent his formative years in the country on his grandfather's farm. He lived in Vermont until his sixteenth year and then, at the end of his junior year in high school, his father moved the whole family out of the snow belt and into the sunshine of Phoenix, Arizona, where Dave raised his three children and worked in the printing industry for 28 years. Most of his spare time, when he wasn't playing coach to his children's many soccer, baseball and football teams, was spent teaching carving seminars and perfecting his art.

Dave presently resides in Scottsdale, Arizona, and has been a full-time woodcarving instructor, artist and show judge since 1996. He has won countless awards for his carvings across the country. He is available to teach seminars and has created a number of original design wood roughouts and casted study aids, which are available for sale.

For information about seminars in your area or purchasing roughouts and study aids, please contact Dave at the following address:

Dave Stetson
Stetson Woodcarving
5629 E. Sylvia Street
Scottsdale, AZ 85254
480–367–9630
Email: Lcnmichele@aol.com
http://stetsoncarving.com

Preface

Perhaps I should have first completed a figure for the book and then stayed true to that piece, but that's not the way that I carve. Each time that I start a figure, I want to allow myself the option to change or modify the figure as my mind or mood so dictates.

To be creative, I believe we must allow ourselves the opportunity to create. This does not mean that we don't need to be disciplined to be true to our subject, given the anatomy, mood, attitude and movement that must prevail. It also does not mean that we don't need to be true to the principles of form, perspective, structure and clean cuts, for those will make the difference between a good carving and a bad carving.

The creative process involves more the freedom to make changes and try new approaches and the ability to see our subject, not only from a different view or angle, but also from a different attitude or a different mood. Often, at least for me, this means seeing the subject from another artist's perspective. Analyzing what or how another carver or sculptor or artist sees will open doors to give each of us a new perspective or outlook on the world around us. We may not even like the way a subject is presented to us, but that can often afford an even more enlightening view because our mind will not be clouded or encumbered by the overwhelming satisfaction and enjoyment derived from a pleasurable experience.

I generally like to let my figures just happen. This means that I like to go with the flow, allowing my mood at the time to dictate the direction in which the figure will grow. I like to build on each element and work with whatever presents itself. For those who have trouble carving in this manner, try to learn more about your subject. Once you know your subject, you're not limited.

And so it is with the writing of this book. It is my hope that you, the reader, will use this book as an inspiration to open up your creative side. This book should not be used as a step-by-step guide that is limited in its scope, but rather as a guide to inspire and to encourage creativity, for creativity is the keystone of caricature. I hesitated to do a book with a step-by-step approach for fear that it may inhibit the carver's ability to create original pieces of his own. I see so much work that is copied from other carvers "how-to books." As much as you have the ability to copy from another carver, you also have the ability to create your own original work. You just have to do it. You have to go for it and not be afraid to make mistakes, for mistakes are the doors of opportunity to learn.

You will make mistakes, but the mistake only involves a piece of wood and the time that you have involved in it. If you turn that mistake into a learning experience and add it to the next piece that you do, you will start to develop a style that is your own. You may take something from another carver, or something from me or this book, or something from your own mistakes and your own experiences in life around you, and all of that will be incorporated into your carving style; because, what goes into your brain, comes out your fingertips. Your hands and fingers are tools of the mind, and they can only perform what the mind knows. You will develop a style that is strictly yours and yours alone. My style changes from month to month and from year to year. I believe that it is impossible to not change your style, unless you crawl into a hole and don't associate with the world, because it all becomes part of you.

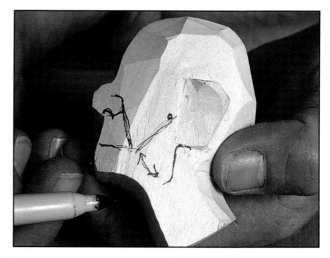

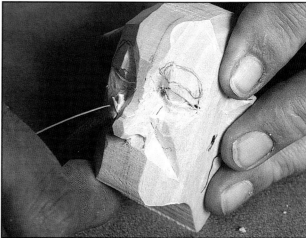

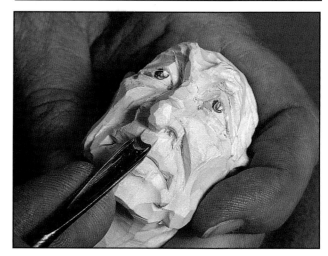

Use this book to master the technique of caricature carving; then use it to inspire the creativity within you. Creativity is the keystone of caricature.

Chapter One

Mastering the Art of Caricature Carving

Caricature carving has always been included in a category with cartoon carving, probably because there has never been a distinction between the carving styles with regard to carving competitions. Unfortunately, because of this, the general perception of the public has been that cartoon is the same as caricature. I would now like to set the record—or at least the record according to Stetson—straight. Caricature by definition is an exaggeration of realism, whereas cartoon can fall into a definition regarded as a distortion of realism. (See Figure 1.)

In caricature, joints bend where they are supposed to bend and the basic units of anatomy are respected. Proportion is known and respected and exaggerated for effect without distortion. Anatomy is respected as are the folds and draperies of clothing.

In cartoon, the arms and legs can flex and bend as if made of rubber, and the figures of animals such as mice, cats, dogs and ducks (not mentioning any particular personalities by name) bear little resemblance to the real thing. We have all seen cartoons where a figure can be bent up like a pretzel, dunked into a bucket of water, thrown "splat" against a wall, and fall to the floor only to miraculously "pop" back to its original shape.

It is important to realize that I believe carving is 95 percent mental. Our hands are tools of the mind. The hands can do anything that the mind knows to tell them to do. No matter what the creative medium may be, we must know and understand the subject in our mind for our hands to be capable of carrying out the appointed task of recreating the subject. I cannot overemphasize that it must be between our ears before it can come out our fingers.

The major elements of attraction are proportion and symmetry. Without proportion and symmetry we are left with a figure that has no natural appeal. There have been many documented research studies that have determined that we, meaning the human animal, by natural instinct, are attracted to those things that have symmetry and proportion, especially when it comes to the human figure. Proportion and symmetry are the two elements to consider when trying to correct a bad carving. By the term "bad" carving, I refer to those carvings we observe and readily know that something is amiss.

Fig. 1

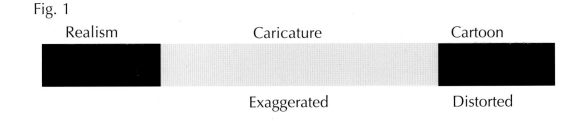

We just can't seem to put our finger on the problem. In the subconscious area of the brain we know when there is a problem, but we don't have ready access to the subconscious for the purpose of analyzing the subject.

For example, we all know what a cow looks like. The image is embedded in our brain. We can all recall this image of a cow, but when we try to use this image to create a likeness of the cow, most of us find that the subconscious image in our brain is insufficient. We don't have a clear picture when we try to analyze the image. It's hard to tell if the horns of the cow are above or below or in front of or behind the ears. How long is the tail in relationship to the hind legs? Is the end of the tail above the hock or below? It soon becomes evident that we must do a little more research to do a proper job of reproducing an image of a cow.

The way we go about this may be to actually observe a cow or perhaps just acquire a photograph or a drawing of the beast. Either way, we must feed information into the conscious part of the brain, for the conscious hemisphere is where the information must be for us to be able to retrieve it to create our image of a cow.

And so it is for anything we want to create. We must know it in the conscious area of the brain in order to use it for creative purposes. The better we know our subject, the more we can feed the tools of the brain (our hands) and the more accurately we can reproduce the subject.

When considering symmetry in our carvings, we don't necessarily want the figures to be exactly the same on the left and right side. Total symmetry can be uninteresting, but interest by way of asymmetry must have balance. In this way, symmetry and balance can be synonymous.

Proportion must be respected to have an image that has appeal. We can exaggerate proportion for effect but we must know what realistic proportions are before we can exaggerate them.

The first and most important element that we as carvers need to notice about the human head is that the head is the basic shape of an egg or oval. The oval is about one third more distant from top to bottom than it is from side to side. The oval of the head is also evident in the top view of the head, and again, it is more distant by about one-third from front to back than it is from side to side.

The side view of the head can be created by two ovals. It is important to notice that the neck aligns with the spine and that the back of the head is about even with the point of the shoulder. Therefore, the head sits out in front of the body and not up on top of the shoulders like a soldier with his chin in and his chest out. This is the basic form and shape that I start with when creating a head on a figure.

We next must determine a head shape, for it is important to first create a head on which to place the features. I have personally wasted the time of many students over the years by trying to teach them the basics of carving facial features on the corner of a stick. The problem is that we have too much difficulty trying to apply those features from the stick to a head. Generally we get the features on the wood and whatever is left over becomes the head shape. I believe that we first need the head shape to make a head look like some particular person.

Some caricature artists, drawing a face, will begin with a feature on the face and work their way out. They can get away with it because the act of drawing allows them to add the head shape after the features are drawn. As woodcarvers, we are forced to work our way into the wood from the outside, thus making it necessary to create the head shape first.

Once we have a head shape, we can begin placing the features on the face where they belong. The placement of the features that I will show are average human proportions. No one in the human race has the perfect average proportions, and for every rule that we have for proportions, there will be someone whose feature placement will break the rules. You will also notice that those individuals who break the rules of average proportions will be those who we find to be less attractive.

Front View

Beginning with the front view of the head, take notice of the following "rules."

Rule 1: The eye line is located about halfway between the top of the head and the bottom of the chin.

Rule 2: The base of the nose is placed halfway between the eye line and the bottom of the chin.

Rule 3: The base of the nose is the place where the nose meets the upper lip, so the actual tip of the nose sits just above the base. It is also important to note that the tip of the nose is a rounded shape.

Rule 4: Halfway between the base of the nose and the bottom of the chin is the location of the bottom of the lower lip. That means the line of the mouth separating the lips is above the halfway mark.

Side View

Moving to the side view of the head, we have a new set of rules. (Placement of the ear is also seen in the front and top view diagrams.)

Rule 1: If we locate a vertical line half way between the front and back of the head, the front edge of the ear will be on that line with the entire ear resting behind the line.

Rule 2: The top edge of the ear will be in line with the brow of the eye.

Rule 3: The attachment point of the top front edge of the ear is in line with the eye line.

Rule 4: The bottom of the ear lobe is in line with the moustache, or somewhere between the nose and the line of the mouth.

Rule 5: The bottom of the ear lobe is probably one of the most variable locations of all the facial features.

Now that we know where the features are supposed to be located on a realistic head, we can think about moving them for an exaggerated effect, which is a beginning for exercising the rights of caricature. Remember that caricature is an exaggeration of realism. We can move features around on the head to exaggerate proportions, but we must respect the features relationships to each other. Distorting the features' relationships to each other will result in an unattractive or ugly head. In the first figure, we show normal realistic feature placement. In the second figure, we raise the features placement on the head to suggest a strong chin. In the third figure we lower the placement to suggest a strong head or intelligent look.

These principles will become more and more apparent as we work through lessons on anatomy and expressions and a caricature carving demonstration.

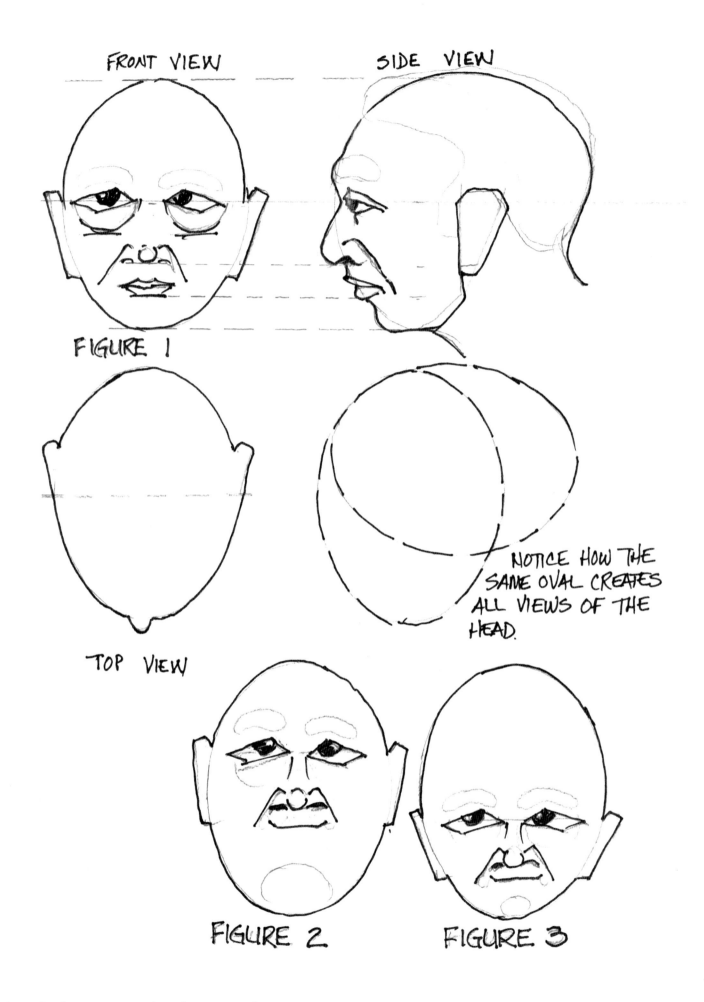

FRONT VIEW

SIDE VIEW

FIGURE 1

TOP VIEW

NOTICE HOW THE SAME OVAL CREATES ALL VIEWS OF THE HEAD.

FIGURE 2

FIGURE 3

Chapter Two

Using and Caring for a Carving Knife

Figure 1 A wide array of carving knives is available. Find a quality knife that suits your style.

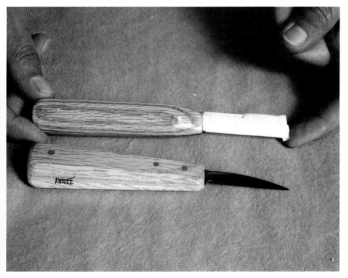

Figure 2 Knife handles can be altered to fit your hand. The bottom knife shows an unaltered handle; the handle of the top knife has been altered.

Carving knives come in a wide variety of styles, shapes and various degrees of quality. (See Figure 1.) As a general rule of thumb, you get what you pay for. Usually, the more a knife costs, the better the steel in the blade is; however, fancy handles can drive up the cost and not make the blade any better. So, choice then becomes a matter of personal preference.

I like to have a blade that cuts on the straight edge as opposed to one that cuts on the curved edge. I also prefer a handle that feels the same in my hand whether I'm cutting toward myself or away from myself. Also, when my knife wears out from repeated sharpening (about every year or so), I get a new knife, so I generally avoid fancy handles.

When I purchase a new knife, I sometimes need to modify the handle to better fit my hand. (See Figure 2.) In this case, the bottom knife is an example of a handle as it comes from the maker that is unacceptable for my use. I need to round off the handle so it fits better in my fingers. Before working on the knife handle, I first want to protect myself from the blade by covering it with several layers of masking tape so I won't be cutting myself. After modifying the handle, I can hold the knife comfortably in my fingers and have less stress and fatigue when carving. (See Figure 3.)

Over the years, I have acquired a large collection of equipment to help me sharpen my tools. Initially, none of them worked. Each time I learned of a new stone, I had to get it, thinking that it would be the magic answer to my dull knife problems. After months of trying different methods and materials to get a sharp knife, I finally found the answer, or so I thought. Actually, they all work. My problem was simply my inexperience. Practice with what you have. It will work when you get the knack, and the knack will come to you with practice.

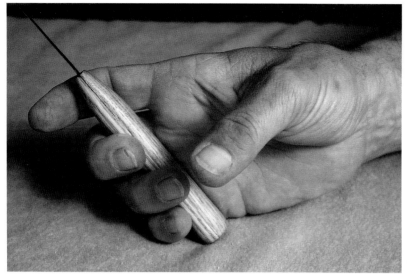

Figure 3 Once altered, a carving knife should fit comfortably in your hand.

Two Basic Cuts

To make a basic pull cut, pull the blade through the wood by closing the hand. Do not cut by pulling with your wrist or forearm. Strive to maintain control.

For a push cut, place the thumb of the hand that holds the wood against the back of the knife handle. With the other hand, pull back on the knife handle. The thumb acts as a fulcrum against which the knife pivots.

How to Sharpen a Knife

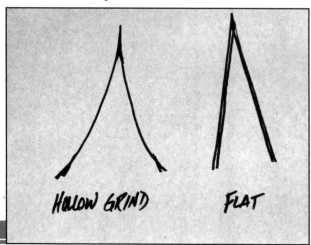

1

Blades are either hollow ground or flat. Hollow ground blades are easier to sharpen because you don't need to remove as much metal as on a flat blade to get a sharp edge.

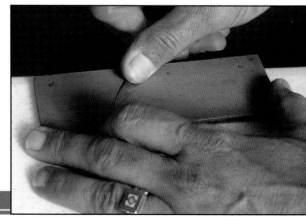

2

To sharpen your knife, you must keep the blade flat to the stone and you need to be as mechanical as possible. In this photo, I am using an E-Z-Lap diamond sharpener.

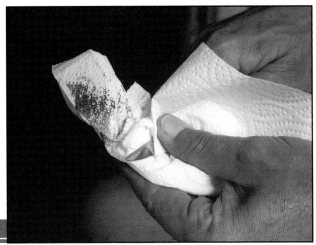

You need no oil or water to use diamond stones, and they clean up with a dry paper towel. The dark material is the metal that the stone removed from the knife.

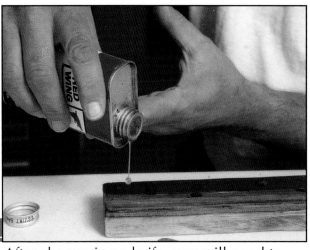

After sharpening a knife, you will need to strop for a fine edge. I prepare my strop—a piece of leather glued to a block of pine—by applying a few drops of leather oil.

Work the oil into the strop and wipe away any excess.

Scrape sharpening compound onto your strop with an old knife. I prefer ZAM, a lapidary compound for polishing stones. The oil helps the compound adhere to the leather.

Keeping the blade flat to the strop, drag the blade backward across the strop, several times on each side of the blade. This action will strop your knife.

A groove cut into one side accepts smaller gouges. The groove allows the gouge to maintain more contact with the surface of the strop.

Carving Technique – Some Do's and Don'ts with a Knife

Photo A is an example of how NOT to carve. First of all, it should be said that most accidents and cuts to the flesh are a result of careless inattention and that most often happens when we are tired. Many are the times when I have thought I'm feeling a little tired now but I'm going to make one last cut before I quit. Of course that is the very moment when I apply too much pressure to the knife and cut myself. It does, however, become the last cut of the session since I'm retrieving a bandage to stop the leak. This push stroke shows the left hand holding the wood and the right hand, wrist and forearm pushing the knife through the wood (very dangerous). When the knife cuts out of the wood, all the pressure and tension exerted by the carver will be suddenly released, resulting in an explosive uncontrolled surge. The sharp blade jumping out of control will most likely cut anything in its way. Often that can result in ruining a good pair of pants or, worse yet, what may lie beneath.

Photo B shows a controlled push cut. The thumb of the hand that is holding the wood is used as a fulcrum at the back of the knife handle close to the blade. The hand holding the knife is literally pulling back on the handle and the leverage against the thumb causes the blade to cut through the wood.

Photo C shows a controlled pull cut. Holding the knife handle in the fingers makes this cut. The knife is pulled through the wood by a gripping motion from the fingers clenching in toward the hand. It is important to keep the thumb of the gripping hand and all parts of the holding hand away from the path of the blade.

Photo A

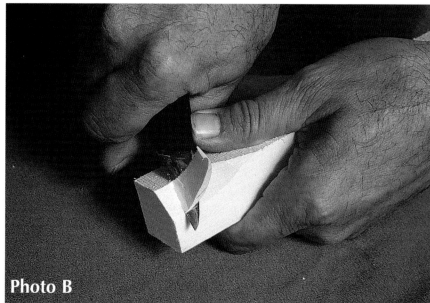

Photo B

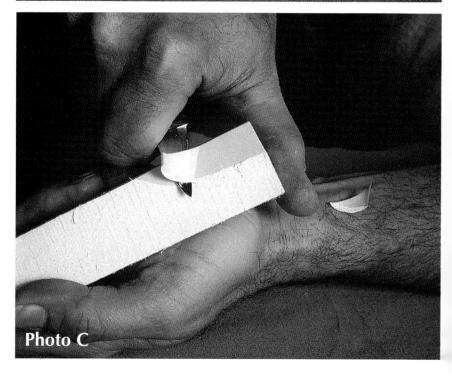

Photo C

Tools

Chapter Three

Anatomy of the Head and Neck

It is truly imperative that we learn anatomy to effectively create good caricature. The better we know and understand our subject, the better prepared we are to create it. Often, we know in our subconscious mind, that something is wrong, but we don't know how to correct it because we don't know the subject in our conscious mind. Most of us cannot pull information to create from our subconscious. So to feed that knowledge into the conscious mind, it must be learned.

I have found that one of the best ways to study the anatomy of a head and neck is to model it in clay. On the following pages you will see how I use clay to form the head, from the skeleton out.

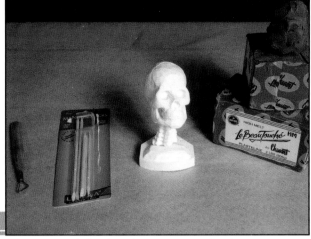

1

The materials that I use to study the anatomy are a clay loop tool, manicure sticks, skull model and plasteline clay.

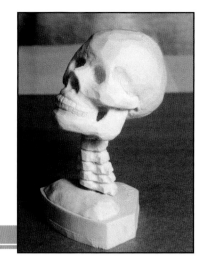

2

The skull model is molded and cast from a carving that I created. Included are the seven cervical vertebrae that connect the skul to shoulders.

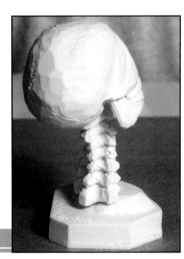

3

A back view shows how the vertebrae attach to the lower side of the skull.

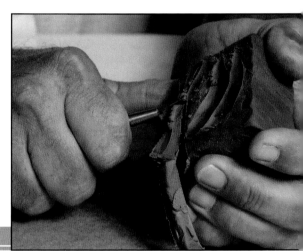

4

Begin by creating smaller pieces of clay th can be warmed in your hand to make ther more pliable.

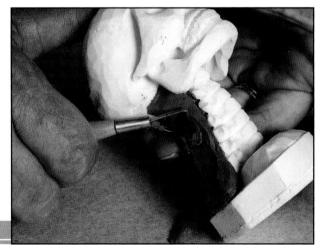

5

If the clay muscles that are added to the skull are too large, you can carve them smaller with the loop tool. I begin with the large trapezius muscles at the back of the neck.

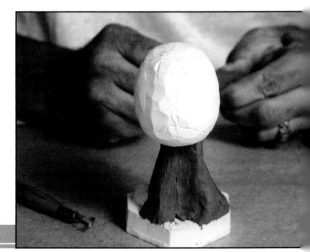

6

Whatever muscle is applied to one side is repeated on the other side. Try to keep th muscles as symmetrical as possible.

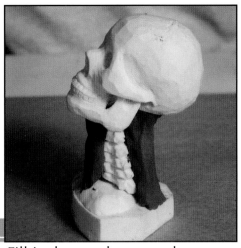

7 Fill in the esophagus or throat area.

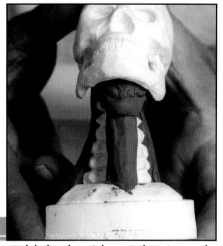

8 Add the hyoid or Adam's apple to the throat.

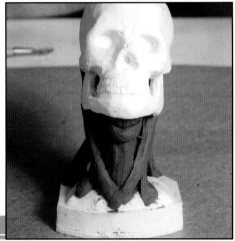

9 Add the sternomastoid muscles from the skull, just behind the jawbone, to the base of the neck.

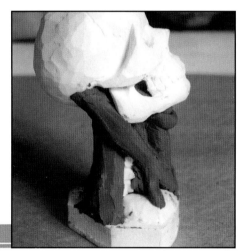

10 Here you can see a side view of the major neck muscles.

11 Add the eyeballs and nose.

12 Notice how the eyeballs and nose protrude from the skull. They will be less noticeable after finishing the facial construction.

Add the masseter muscles that operate the jaw and the orbicularis, or brow, and the frontalis muscle that lifts the brow.

13

14

This photo show a side view of th jaw and eyebrow muscles.

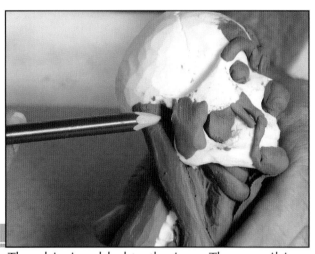

15

The chin is added to the jaw. The pencil is pointing to the location of the ear canal, or hole in the ear, so we know where to locate a wedge of clay for the ear.

16

Attach the ear.

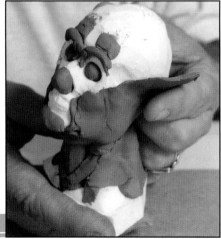

17

Now begin to flatten out some clay to use as skin to cover the major muscle groups and skull.

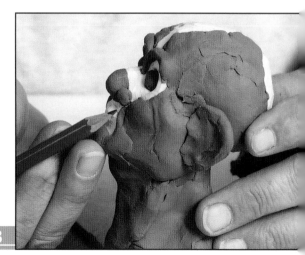

18

Two small balls of clay are added to the si of the nose for the nostrils.

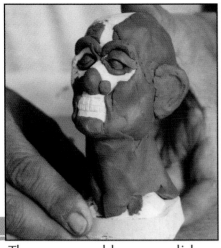

19

The upper and lower eyelids are added to the eyeball, then the remaining skin is added to the face.

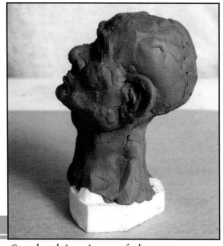

20

Study this view of the completed left side.

21

This photo shows the back view.

22

The right side is complete except for the final layer of skin.

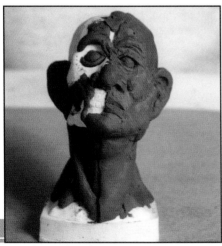

23

Look at the front view, comparing the finished half of the head with the unfinished half.

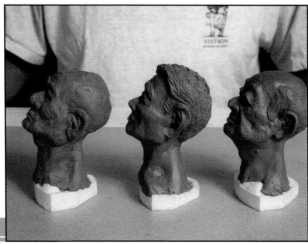

24

In this photo you'll see the side view of finished head, a finished head with hair added, and a finished head showing the aging process.

Chapter Four

Carving a Face with Expression

This chapter will deal with what I refer to as a "practice stick." The carving is not intended to be a completed or finished carving for display; rather, it is a "working sketch" from which a carver can gain insight into the process for laying out the forms that are used to represent a face in the wood. Practice never makes perfect, only perfect practice can lead you in that direction. None of us are capable of perfection, but we can all practice to gain improvement. The block of wood that I use for this exercise is $1^1/2"$ square and does for the woodcarver what a sketchbook does for the flat artist. Regular practice reproducing images that you have observed will lead to improvement.

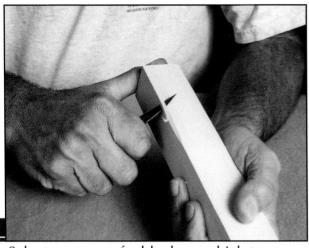

Select a corner of a block on which to carve the face. Begin by removing the corner of the block. This is where the tip of the nose will be, and we don't want a sharp point.

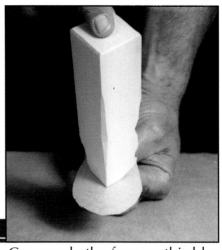

Carve only the face on this block. By placing a template for a full head against the end of the stick, there is no wood for the back of the head because the block is square.

The second step is to cut the profile of the nose, brow and chin into the corner of the block.

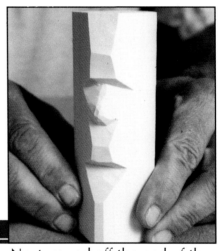

Next, round off the end of the nose. When making a round shape from a squared shape, begin by removing the corners. The bridge of the nose is angled up to the brow.

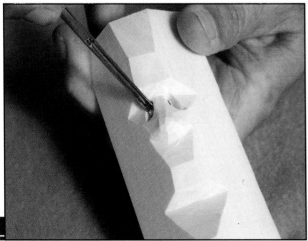

I establish the bridge of the nose with a small veiner so as to not remove the wood that I will need to create a mound for the eye.

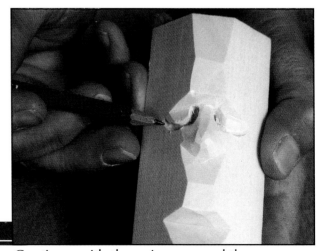

Continue with the veiner around the eye mound. The lower edge of the mound extends about halfway down the nose to the cheekbone. Using a knife, round the eye mound.

Caricature Carving from Head to Toe • 17

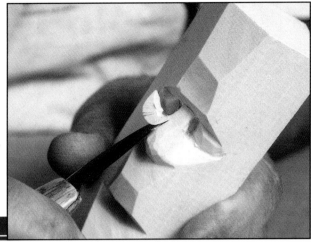

7

Slide the knife along the cheekbone, curving up along the edge of the nose.

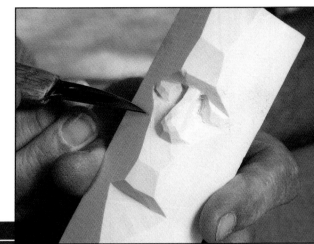

8

The results will allow you to determine how wide or how narrow you want the nose to be

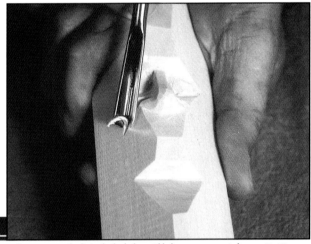

9

The nasolabial fold will be cut with a "V" tool. Begin at the top of the nostril and cut down to the edge of the mouth.

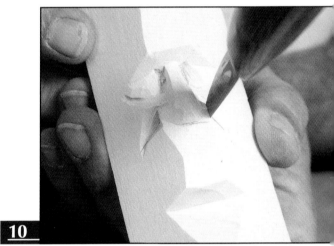

10

Remove a triangular chip from the side of the nostril. This cut will seemingly lift the nose from the face.

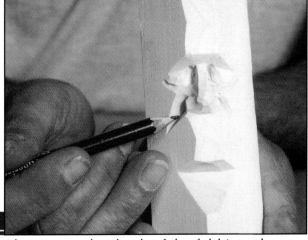

11

The greater the depth of the fold into the face, the older the face will appear.

12

Layout the upper eyelid. Notice how the shape of the lid, from inside corner to outside, travels in an upward direction for one third of the distance and then drops down for the final two thirds.

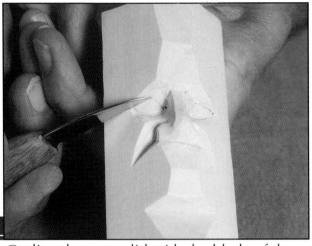

13 Outline the upper lid with the blade of the knife. Cut to a depth equaling the thickness of an eyelid. A deeper cut will make the lids weak and susceptible to breakage.

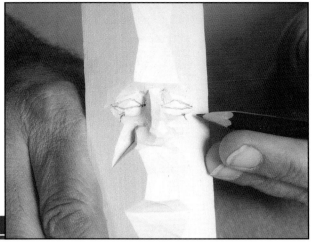

14 Thin the eye mound up to the edge of the upper eyelid and layout the lower lid. Notice that the shape of the lower lid is the reverse of the upper.

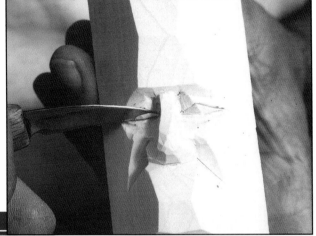

15 Finish exposing the eyeball by trimming the mound from the upper lid down and in to the lower lid. Be careful not to carve away the mound that you have worked so hard to create.

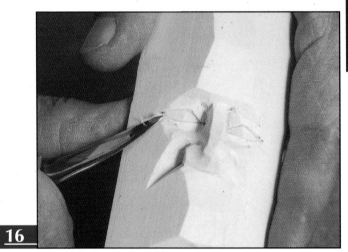

16 Extend the upper lid at the outside corner and tuck the lower lid under the upper.

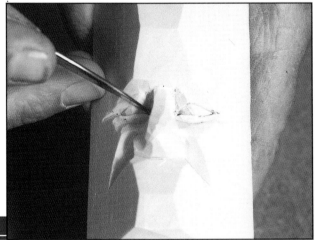

17 Using the tip of the knife cut a small chip from the inside corner of the eye to create the illusion of a tear duct. This will also add extra depth and interest to the eye.

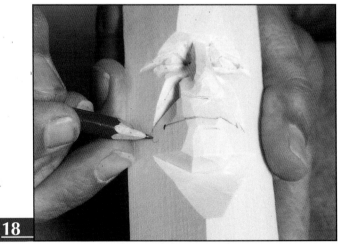

18 Draw in the line of the mouth separating the lips. Notice that the corner of the mouth will not touch the nasolabial fold.

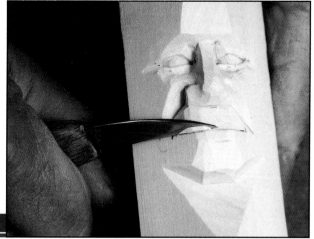

19

Make an angled cut along the upper lip, down and in to the stop cut. This cut will be made twice on each side of the mouth with the cuts connecting in the middle.

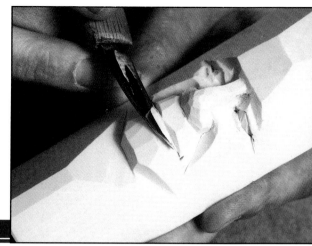

20

On the center of the lower lip, make a cut up and in to the bottom of the upper lip.

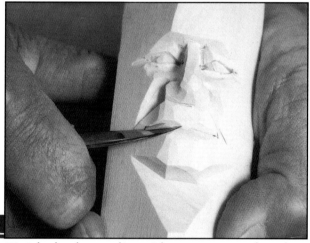

21

Finish the lower lip with a cut on each side of the center cut.

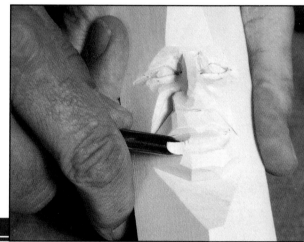

22

Using a gouge, outline the lower edge of th lower lip, stopping against the upper lip at the corner of the mouth.

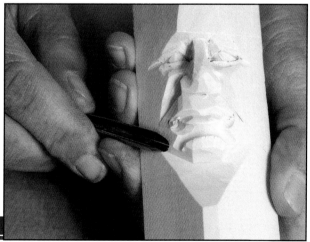

23

From the gouge cut that outlined the lower lip, extend the gouge down and around the chin.

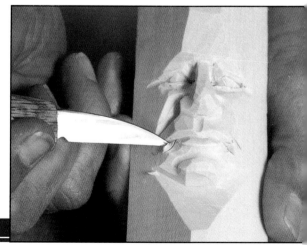

24

Using the tip if the knife, remove a small triangular chip from the corners of the mou

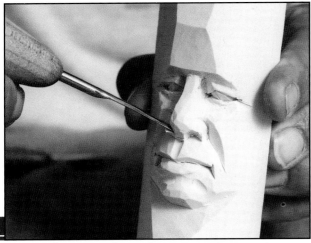

25 Open the nostrils with a curved cut using the tip of the knife.

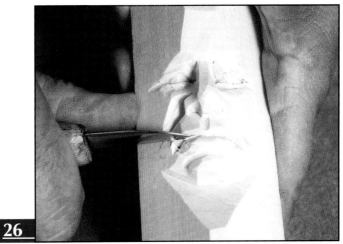

26 Outline the edge of the upper and lower lips with the tip of the knife.

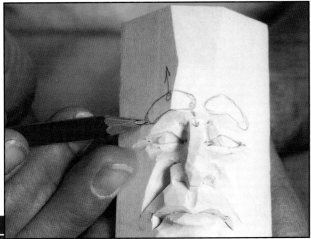

27 The shape and direction of the brow will indicate the expression of the eye. Pulling up the center of the brow will wrinkle the forehead and help to create a pleasant expression. Pulling the inside edge of the brow down will create a determined or angered expression.

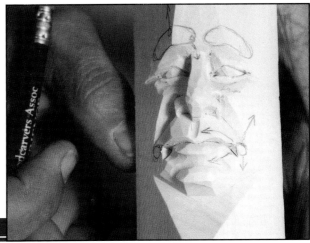

28 The corner of the mouth can pull the lips to the center for whistling, kissing or blowing. The corners can pull back and up for a smile or down for a grimace.

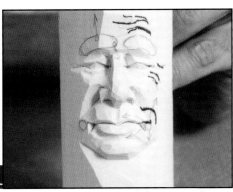

29 When the corner of the mouth or the brow is pulled, it will cause the adjoining flesh to wrinkle at the pull. Pulling up the cheek will also cause crows feet wrinkles along the cheekbone under the outside corner of the eye.

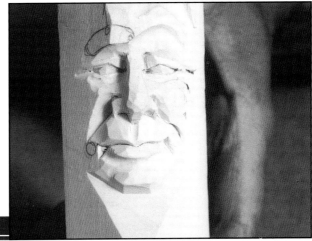

30 The carved result is a smile as seen on the left side of the face.

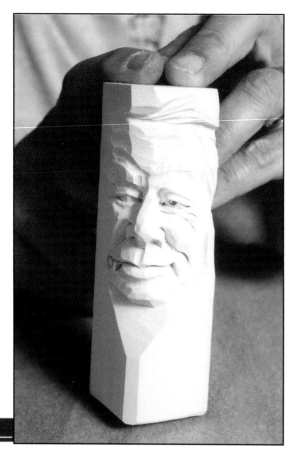

31

Now we will outline the brow on the right side of the face for a frown using a gouge.

32

Pulling down on the corner will finish the expression. Use a gouge to outline the muscle at the corner of the mouth. If the results look confusing, try covering one half of the face.

Chapter Five

Carving the Old Man

Carving requires knowledge of the subject. Ninety percent of all carving takes place between the ears. Without full knowledge of the subject, you're no better off than the "good ol' boy" sittin' on the porch makin' a point on the end of a stick. Your hands are "tools of the mind" and they can only perform tasks the mind knows because they are controlled by the mind. It's impossible, using our hands, to properly create a subject without knowledge of that subject.

Researching the subject by means of studying the subject live or through books in the library will prepare us with the knowledge required to begin carving. One of the ways we have to compile information on a subject is to create the subject in clay. The clay manikin then becomes our model of reference from which to work. Using the medium of plasteline clay allows us to add and remove and add again until we reach the desired look for our figure. Because the clay will not dry, we can use it over and over again.

The amount of detail that goes into a model varies by your own requirements and your prior knowledge of the subject matter. In other words, you may be comfortable with creating the head and face, so you may not spend a lot of effort in that area, rather devoting your efforts to the movement of the body or the folds in the clothing.

The initial investment for the clay is minimal and well worth the money and time when you consider the savings in wood and time by working out problems before they become insurmountable.

The brand of clay that I prefer is called Le Beau Touché (the beautiful touch) by Chavant. It is a high melt product, as living in Phoenix can turn normal plasteline clay into a molten mess in the summer. However, any clay product will work just fine.

We'll begin with a "pinch model," which is just a small figure about the size of your hand. This is similar to a "thumbnail" sketch for a flat artist. Being small, the figure will not require an armature to hold its shape and it will be very easy to set and move elements for proportion and movement. Once refinements are complete on the smaller pinch model, the model can be enlarged and refined in greater detail if so desired; however, creating a larger model may require the use of an armature to help the clay hold its shape. Simple armatures can be made of wood, wire, pipe and Styrofoam or any combination or all of the mentioned items.

Shaping the Body

Take Note:

Some things to consider: The hand hanging at rest is at mid thigh, the size of the hand is equal the size of the face (wrist to fingertip is same as from chin to hairline) and foot (wrist to fingertip is equal to the distance from heal to ball of foot or foot minus the toes) The arms and legs can be suggested as cylinders.

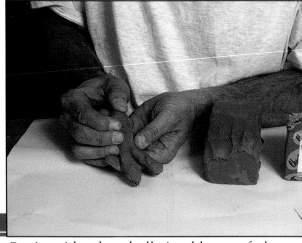

Begin with a baseball-sized lump of clay, pinch and form your figure to create a very basic shape for a torso, then attach the head, arms and legs.

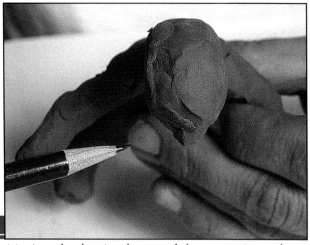

Notice the basic shape of the torso is wider from side to side than from front to back. The head is just the reverse: one third more distant from front to back than from side to side.

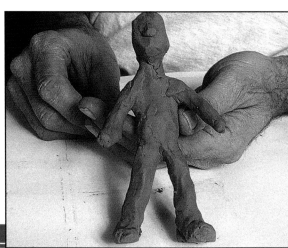

The basic figure should appear something like the figure in the photo. The clay figure is not finished; at this point we are striving for good proportion.

Take Note:

Caricature by definition is an exaggeration of realism. Therefore, we can exaggerate actual proportions but we want joints to bend where they're supposed to bend and we usually need to establish limits to their range of motion. It's also important to remember that for most every rule that I give, you will find an exception to that rule. But these rules remain true: The head is more distant from front to back than from side to side and the torso is more distant from side to side than from front to back (unless you have a very large belly). Just don't use the "exception" clause as a cop out to not learn the correct way that we are made.

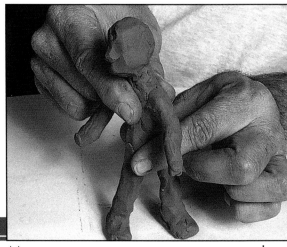

Now we can create some movement by turning or twisting the spine, or torso.

Take Note:

If we carved snakes the same way that most of us carve the human figure, we would end up with nothing more than a straight stick with a head on it. Snakes bend, coil and move. We also bend, coil and move by means of the spine. We don't necessarily have the same flexibility as a snake, but our spine can move in much the same way. The movement in the spine is where we get the major movement or animation in a figure. We can bend forward and backward. We can turn shoulders left and right opposing our hips. We can dip our shoulders left and right. We can turn our torso one direction and turn our head the opposite way creating a twist in our spine at the neck. We have a full range of motion. If anything happens to limit range of motion, it is immediately evident to anyone observing that person, that they have a problem. Therefore, limiting the natural motion in your figure makes it immediately evident that something is wrong to anyone observing your figure.

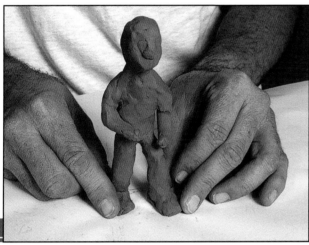

5 Position one foot in front of the other and bend the arms at the elbows and shoulders. Be aware of balance so that the figure doesn't appear to be falling over.

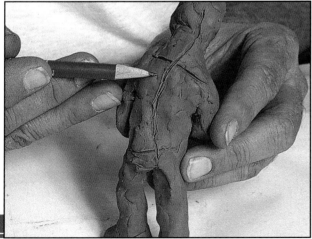

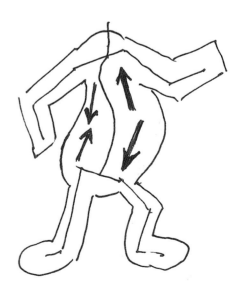

6 Tilt the hips and shoulders toward or away from each other, and turn or tilt the head. This movement involves the spine, which is centered down the back of the figure, running from the head to the hips.

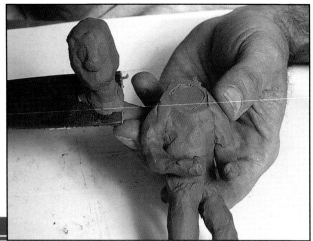

7

Remove the head to prepare the torso, arms and legs for drawing a template. We will create a head and hands separately from the figure and add them on later.

8

Using a combination square or any right angle device, place the clay model on its side, back and front to outline the figure. This will create a pattern for band sawing.

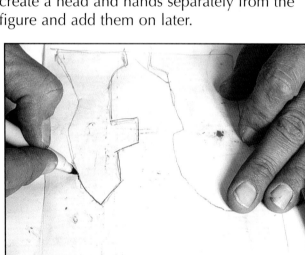

9

I like to transfer the paper pattern to clear Mylar. There are a variety of sources where Mylar can be obtained. One source is the packaging that many products are sold in.

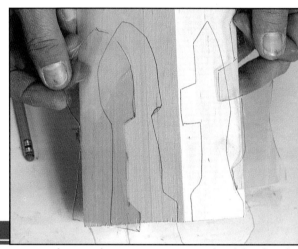

10

Trace the Mylar pattern onto the block of basswood.

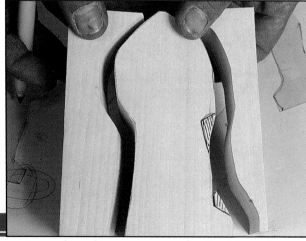

11

Using a band saw, cut out both sides of one view.

12

Reattach the two cut off pieces with spot tacks from a hot melt glue gun. You will now have a square block to cut out the second view.

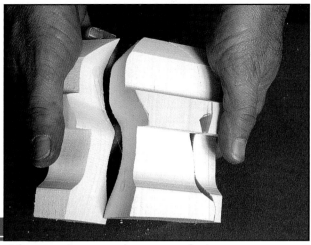

13

After cutting out the second view, you can easily pop off the glue tacked pieces.

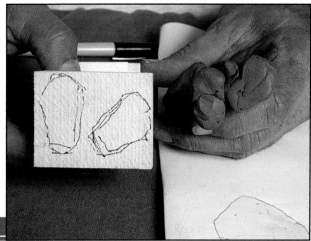

14

Now it's time to block in the body, arms and legs. Referring to your clay model, draw an outline for the bottom of the feet. The right foot is slightly turned and ahead of the left.

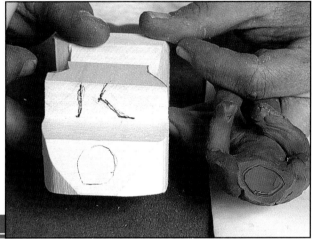

15

Referring to your clay model, draw an outline for the top of the arms. The left arm comes out from the body and the right arm comes across the body.

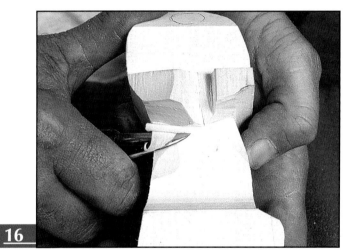

16

The carving process will block in the major forms of the figure without much regard for detail. Details can be added with just a few shallow cuts if you first shape the major form.

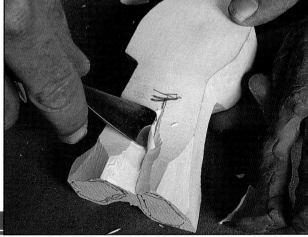

17

Remove material from behind the right leg and between the back of the legs. Carve around the feet.

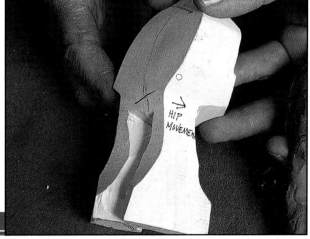

18

Referring to the clay model, notice that the right hip will rotate forward.

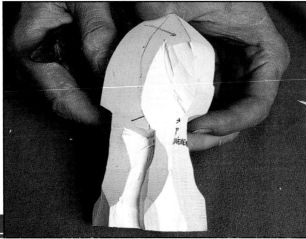

19

Remove material from the hip and torso behind the right arm. This will rotate the right hip forward and take advantage of the spine's flexibility.

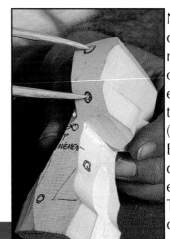

20

Next I break the figure down into six points of movement: three on top of the figure (shoulder, elbow and wrist) and three on the bottom (hip, knee and ankle). Begin by drawing a quarter-inch circle at each of the points. Then, using a pair of dividers, make sure the measurements are equal on both sides. At this point, the actual length of each dimension is unimportant. It only matters that the left and right sides are the same.

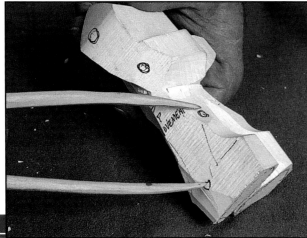

21

Locate the points of the hip, knee and ankle, and using a pair of dividers, check to be sure that the left and right sides are equal.

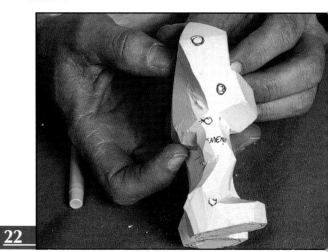

22

Carve the legs into cylinders that bend at the knee. Set the ankle and block in the foot.

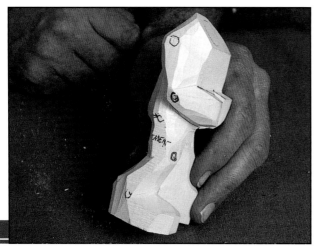

23

Carve the arms into cylinders that bend at the elbow. Set the wrist and block in the hands, unless the hands are to be carved separately as we are doing here.

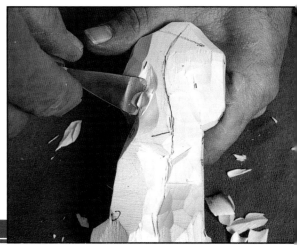

24

Shape the body and give the spine an "S" curve if possible. The more we move the spine, the more natural movement we create.

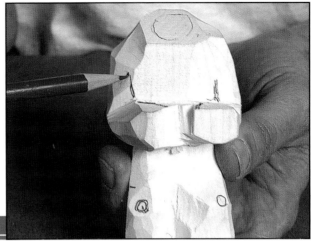

25

Indicate where the upper arm will be separated from the body.

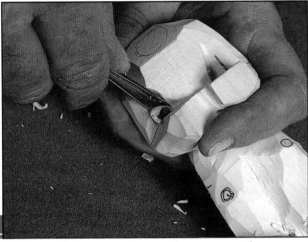

26

Using a "V" or parting tool, separate the upper arm from the body. Note that the more we separate the arms and legs the more fragile the carving is. It is important to have as much extremity contact as possible with the body.

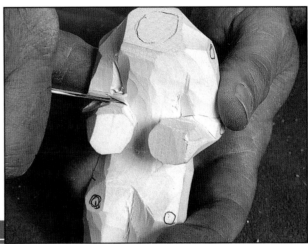

27

Using a knife, continue the process of making cylinders of the arm segments. Note that the armpit is only halfway between the elbow and shoulder. Most carvers tend to set the armpit way too high on the shoulder.

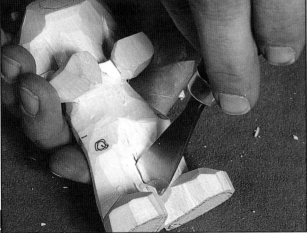

28

Separate the front side of the legs removing the front of the left leg.

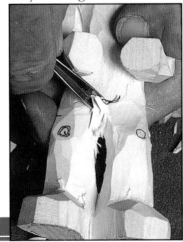

29

Indicate the shape of the crotch and continue to open up the area between the legs. Note that the crotch is about halfway between the knee and the point of the hip. Remember, we will be carving to positive shape and form. Do not attempt to carve a hole, rather carve around the right and left leg and a separation or hole will be the result. If your goal is to carve a hole, it will most likely be in the wrong place.

Carving the Head

I'm often asked, "How do you select a block of wood and how do you know what's good wood for carving and what wood should I avoid?" The wood I prefer for carving is American linden or basswood. It grows primarily in the north central and northeastern United States.

The wood needs to be cut during the coldest winter months when the tree in dormant and sap is not running. It also needs to be milled and stacked for drying before the spring temperatures begin to rise. Summer cut has too much sap, and logs that are left lying around can develop spalting and blue streak. The whiter the wood, the better I like it, because it seems to provide a better base for finishing. Darker or "honey" colored basswood gives a darker finish and requires more work to achieve the desired colors in the finished carving.

Fresher cut wood will have better moisture content, and older wood will be dryer and more difficult to cut. If someone has wood at a bargain price that has been seasoned for several years in his or her garage, I will avoid it. As it dries, the cells in the wood contract and become very hard. As far as I know, trying to rehydrate the wood will only result in wet wood with tight cells and your wood will most probably mildew, especially if kept in a plastic bag. Good, fresh basswood is not all that expensive and will save you many hours of frustration.

Carving

1

Layout the head on a separate block of wood. The head shape as seen from above is egg or oval shaped, more distant from front to back than from side to side. Notice how I have oriented the face of the figure to the outside of the wood grain. I find that this helps in my attempts to achieve symmetry.

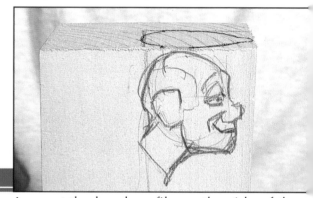

2

Lay out the head profile on the side of the block.

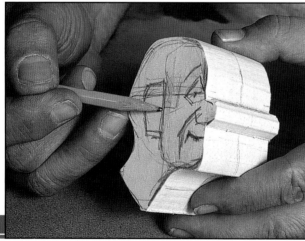

3

Bandsaw the profile of the head. Note that the front edge of the ear is on a vertical plane that equally divides the center of the head.

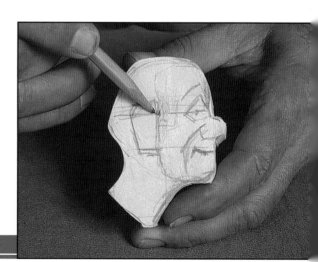

4

The top of the ear is even with the brow and the top front of the ear attaches to the side of the head at a line even with the eye. The bottom of the ear lobe lines up with the are of the face between the nose and mouth or the "moustache."

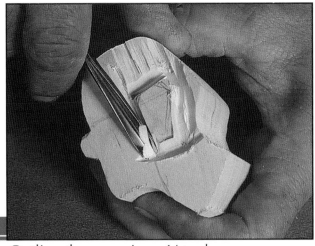

5 Outline the ear using a V tool.

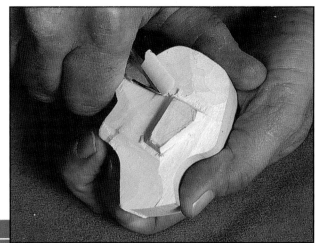

6 Trim away the sides of the head leaving the ear.

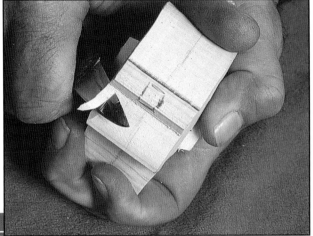

7 Mark the width of the nose and carve an angle on each side of the face to the nose marks.

8 Cut angles rounding over the top and back of the head.

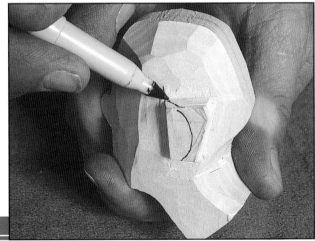

9 Mark an angle to trim the front edge of the ear mass leaving a wedge shape to the ear. The front of the ear is attached to the head and the back edge of the ear sits out away from the head.

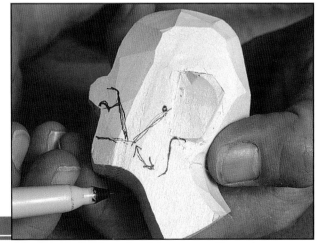

10 Mark up the head with a pencil to show anatomy and to aid you in carving.

Take note:

The marks in Step 10 show where the jaw line drops from the ear and where the end of the nose will be carved. Also indicated are the nasolabial folds that extend down from the upper line of the nostril to the corner of the mouth. A point centered on the front edge of the ear is where the jaw is hinged. If the jaw drops to open the mouth, it will swing back from the hinge, into the neck and the chin will sometimes seem to disappear into the neck. The line from the nose indicates how the nasolabial fold extends back around the dentures to help form a mound in the mouth area; always striving for additional form wherever possible. Notice how the shadow line forming the wing of the nostril always points toward the tip of the nose.

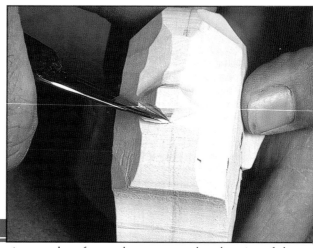

11

A couple of angular cuts under the tip of the nose begin to establish the shape required for carving the nose. When I carve a nose, I first carve that part of the nose that extends out from the face. The nostrils are not a part of the extended section of the nose. The nostrils will be set into the face after establishing the nasolabial fold.

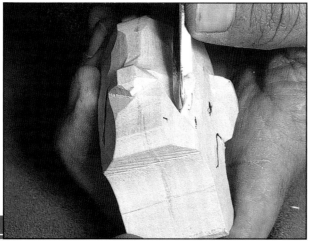

12

The nostrils and nasolabial fold are created with a single curved cut from a V tool.

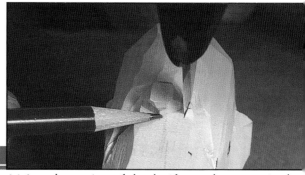

13

Using the point of the knife, make a vertical c straight into the face along the nose or nostril, extending straight down from the nasolabial fold line to a point ending on a horizontal plane even with the base of the nose.

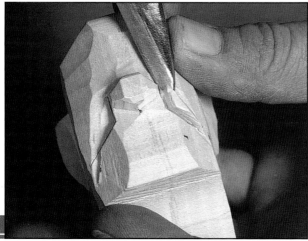

14

Recut the nasolabial fold to remove a three-cornered chip beside the nose to create the wing of the nostril.

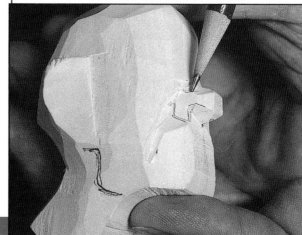

15

This photo shows the completed cut with the chip removed to expose the nostril.

Carving the Eyes

I have always been intrigued with the difficulty that most woodcarvers have when it comes to carving the human eye. Perhaps it's because of the high level of importance that is placed on the eye as an element of expression. Actually the expression of the eye comes from the surrounding tissue of the brow and very little from the eye itself.

Generally speaking, most carvers begin the eye area by first carving a socket. The problem with that approach is that they generally carve off the eyeball and must then recarve the ball so it sets deep into the socket at best or forces the carver to create an eye that is very flat at worst. If we analyze the eye, we will notice a mound or ball, hence, the term "eyeball," not "eyeflat." We are not going to carve "lipid pools of passion" or "windows to the soul," but simply a ball in a socket.

Notice that the exposed portion of the ball can be seen from the side, top, and bottom, as well as from the front. Notice also that the eyelids and the bag under the eye are also formed around the ball. Therefore, our initial efforts should simply be to create the basic form or shape of a ball.

As I observe heads and busts that are created by artists, both present day and those from the past, they don't look like the heads and busts of the average woodcarver. I believe that woodcarvings are relegated to the world of craft and not art because of this very phenomenon. A craft is something handed down from generation to generation and is performed just as it always has been. Art, on the other hand, is an interpretation of the artist's experiences from the world around him.

We must observe the people around us and incorporate what we observe in our carvings so that our work reflects a part of us. Simply copying what we see others doing is perpetuating the denigration of woodcarving to the level of craft rather than art.

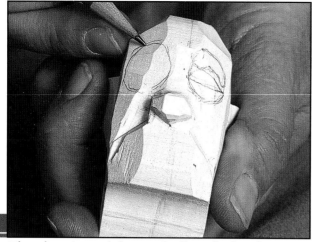

1

The drawing of the eyeball includes the entire ball, even the part of the ball that cannot be seen. This exercise will help you visualize the portion of the ball that we will expose. The drawn ball will encompass the eye, the eyebrow and the bag under the eye.

Take note:

The cut between the eye mound and the nose will be the deepest cut that we make in the face. While making these cuts, keep in mind that we are actually carving the nose and leaving wood for an eye mound. Think of positive shapes and forms that are being left, rather than the holes or negative depressions that are being cut.

Take note:

Two lines represent the shape of the exposed portion of the upper eyelid across the eye mound. First divide the distance from the inside to outside corner of the eye by thirds. Beginning at the inside corner, the line of the lid will travel in an upward direction for one third of the distance and then travel down to the outside corner for the remaining two thirds of the distance.

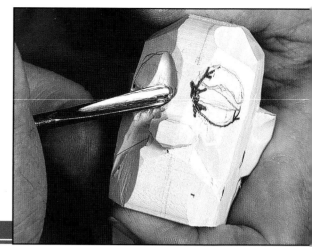

2

Using a small veiner, start with a cut that will separate the bridge of the nose from the eyeball. Notice how the arrows on the uncarved eye indicate the cuts.

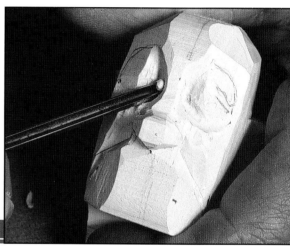

3

Complete the second cut to expose the mound. I have often heard the comment that "If you screw up the carving of an eye, there's always another beneath it." The only thing that is behind the eye is brain matter, so let's get it right the first time.

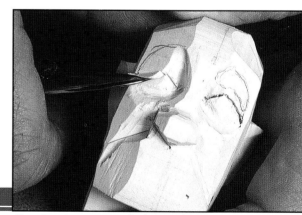

4

Cut in the upper lid. Make a stop cut with the blade of the knife, not the tip. Make the depth of the cuts equal to the thickness of an eyelid. Anything deeper will make the eyelid weak and susceptible to breaking off. Trim the mound up to the stop cut.

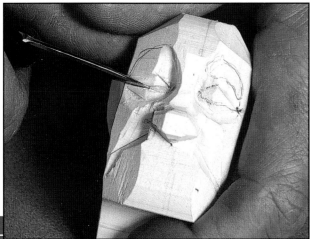

5

The line of the lower lid is the reverse of the upper lid. To cut the lower lid, make a stop cut beginning at the inside corner of the eye and traveling two thirds of the distance to a point just below the outside corner. The final third of the lower lid cut travels from the two-thirds point back up to the outside corner of the eye.

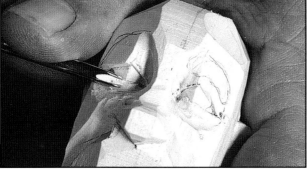

7

Slide your knife along the outside of the lower lid to allow the upper lid to lay on top of the lower lid.

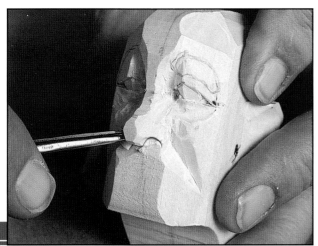

9

To open up the nostril, I use an appropriate sized gouge and stab it straight in under the nose. Do not attempt to pry the chip out with the gouge or you will break off the nostril. Instead, use a knife to cut under the chip and allow the chip to fall out.

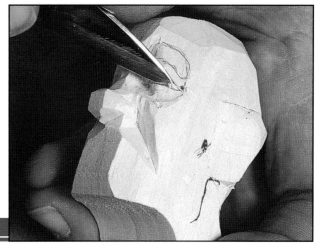

6

Using the tip of the knife, trim the exposed portion of the eye from the edge of the upper lid, down and in to the edge of the lower lid. Be careful not to flatten the eye mound.

8

Slide the knife along the cheek, curving up onto the nose. This cut will establish the width of the nose between the tip and the bridge.

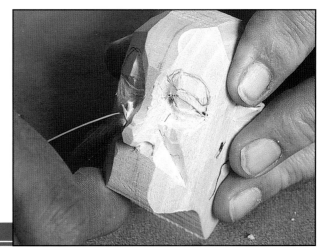

10

Define the shadow of the nostril. The ball at the tip of the nose and the nostrils can be any size , but the shadow between the two always points back toward the tip of the nose.

Caricature Carving from Head to Toe • 37

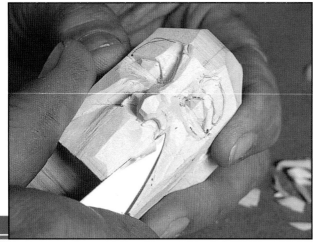

11

Round off the mouth or denture mound.

Take note:

We can deepen the nasolabial fold, if desired. Th[e] deeper the fold, the older the face will appear. The area of the cheek and all areas of the face where we have fatty tissue on the surface are where our appearances are most different. The area of the face where the bone of the skull is close to the surface is where we are most alike. Knowing this makes it easier to evaluate a person[‘s] appearance. These regions are what we need to observe to determine what makes someone look the way they do and what makes them look uniquely different from others. The more we stud[y] faces, the more we notice about people and the more we feed the conscious area of the brain wit[h] useful creative information.

Carving the Mouth

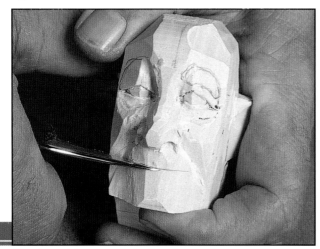

1

Begin with a straight horizontal stop cut across the denture mound dividing the upper and lower lips. This cut will be closer to the nose than to the chin. Remember that the bottom of the lower lip is approximately halfway between the base of the nose and the chin.

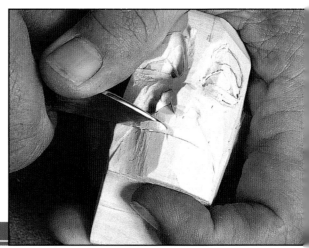

2

The upper lips are formed with a cut angle[d] down to the initial stop cut—one for each of the two halves of the upper lip.

3

The lower lip is formed with three cuts. The first is centered on the lower lip. The knife cut starts just below the lip and travels toward the initial stop cut. Then it slides up and in, ending up under the upper lips.

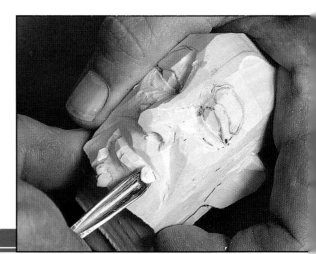

4

Define the lower lip with a 5mm veiner. R[un] a cut from one corner of the mouth to the other, just under the lower lip and followin[g] the lower edge of the lip. The result is a lower lip that is not as wide as the upper lips, but generally thicker.

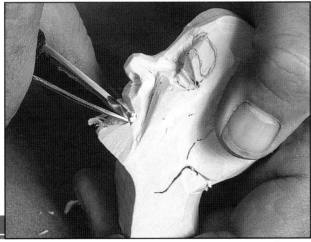

5 Removing a small triangular chip from the corners of the mouth will give added depth and form.

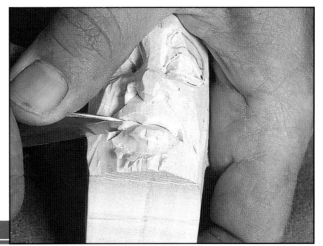

6 Finally we can better define the mouth opening by running the tip of the knife blade along the centerline of the mouth to define the bottom of the upper lip and the top of the lower lip.

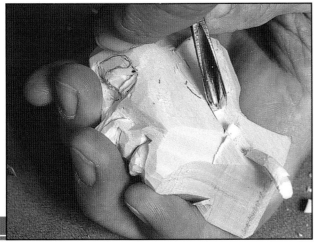

7 Angle the jaw line from the chin to the back edge of the jaw. A gouge cut running down from the bottom of the ear to the neck will indicate the back edge of the jaw.

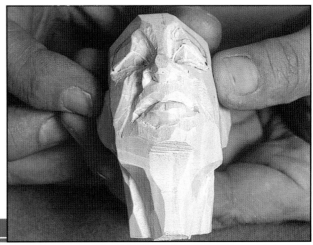

8 Continuing down toward the center of the neck from the back edge of the jaw, on each side, will establish the form for the throat. Do not taper the neck to a round form because you won't be able to establish the neck muscles that hold up the head.

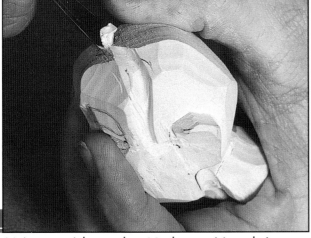

9 Using a wide angle, 60-degree V tool, I now define the outline of the sideburns, hairline and forehead.

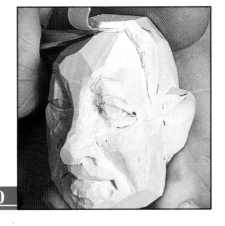

10 Leave the brow and shave the forehead back to the hairline leaving the hair above the plane of the flesh. It is always important to allow plenty of wood for the hair as hair is positive form and always sits above the surface of the head. Never carve the hair into the surface of the flesh.

Caricature Carving from Head to Toe • 39

Detailing the Ear

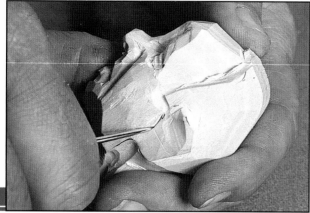

1

After using a large gouge to scoop a cup shape to the upper inside edge of the ear, I use a knife to make a stop cut outlining the tragus.

Take note:

Many caricature carvers set the shape of the tragus with a round gouge, but I have never seen anyone with a round tragus. A round tragus makes the ear look as if it has an earplug inserted into the ear canal. I set the shape more like the view in the drawing.

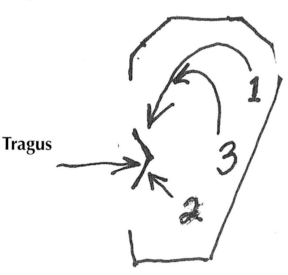

Tragus

2

A 5mm veiner is used to define the inner contour of the ear with a sweeping cut inside the outer edge of the ear ending at the tragus. A second detail cut below the first also ends at the edge of the tragus.

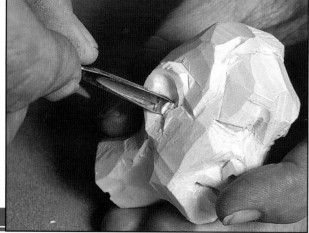

3

Clean out the gouge chips with the knife and round off the edges of the ear. This does not complete the ear.

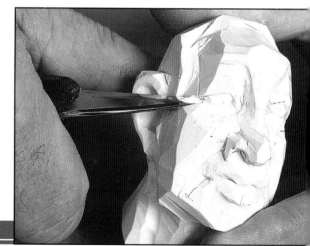

4

Using your knife, extend the upper eyelid and set a small shelf at the top of the cheekbone below the outside corner of the eye. The top of the cheekbone will catch light and create additional form to the cheekbone.

Carving

Take note:

As we work around the head we will revisit the ear for more details. I try to never complete any thing in one stage, rather move around the carving and block everything in and refine shapes and then go back and detail the elements to finish the carving. In other words, I like to allow the carving to grow all together. Moving around the piece and developing the various elements as an entire growing project will help prevent a lot of errors that come to those who carve with tunnel vision.

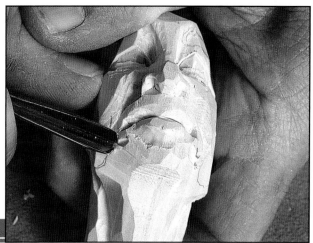

5

Using a gouge or V tool, create some interest in the jowl area of the lower cheek. A V tool will create a harsher line than what you will get with a gouge. Either tool will work; it just depends on the look you like.

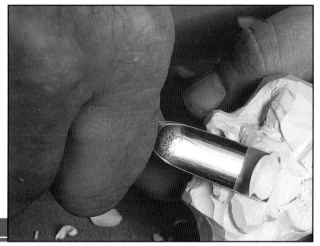

6

A wide shallow gouge (5/8" #5 sweep) can be used to create a deep-set cheek beneath the cheekbone. The more character you add to your face, the older your caricature will appear.

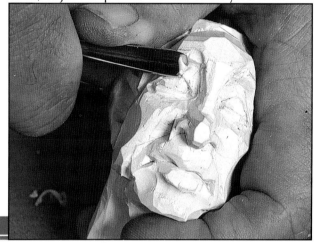

7

Using a V tool, you can create a more deep-set eye by carving between the brow and the eyelid.

Take note:

When creating deep-set eyes, be sure to have the V cut fade to the outside and inside corner of the eye, with the deepest part of the cut at the apex above the eye. Using this technique, you can have a deep-set eye without first carving off the eyeball. This allows the eye to remain more normal looking and still look like a ball with the depth and definition of a real eye.

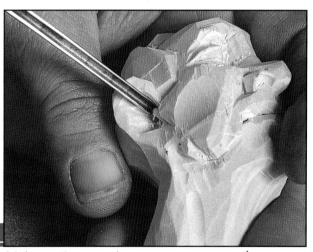

8

Using a 2mm veiner, you can now deepen the negative gouge cuts inside the ear to enhance the positive form that exists within.

Carving the Hair

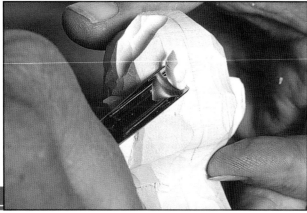

1

Begin the process of carving hair by first showing depth, form and movement with "S" cuts formed by a large gouge flowing in the direction that the hair grows. Be always mindful to carve with the grain knowing that it will most probably change direction as it moves over and around the shape of the head.

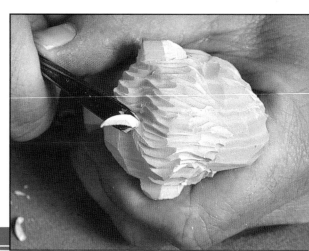

2

Refine the carving of hair by using a smaller veiner to further accent flow and direction of the hair. Look for opportunities to increase shadows by cutting at the top of a predetermined larger gouge cut, thereby darkening the upper extremes of the shadows.

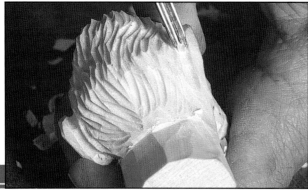

3

Detail and work in even more depth using a finer veiner or V tool.

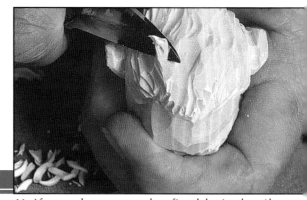

4

Knife work creates the final hair detail.

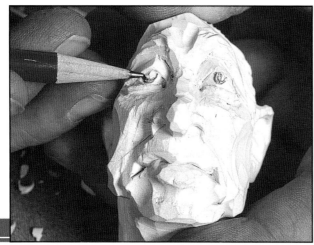

5

Pencil in the eye pupils by drawing a "U" on the eyeball against the upper lid and then filling in one side of the "U" to leave a white spot on the pupil for a highlight.

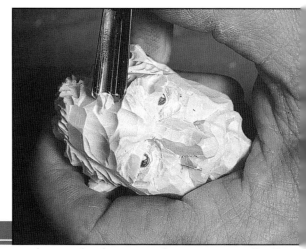

6

Defining the brow with a gouge will allow the brow to be more prominent affording easier access for expressions.

Carving

7

Deepening the nasolabial fold with a knife will further age the face and create more character.

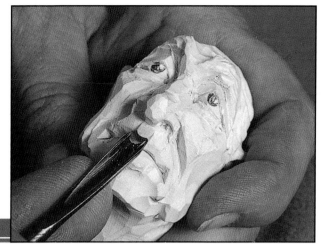

8

Cut the philtrum with a gouge, centered on the upper lip from lip to base of nose.

Carving a Closed Hand

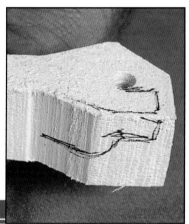

1

Cut out the hand with a band saw using the pattern. Drill a 5/16" hole for the opening. Draw the outline for the thumb. The thumb is going to be drawn around the hole.

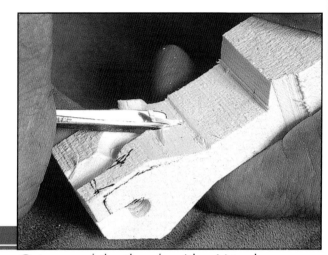

2

Cut around the thumb with a V tool.

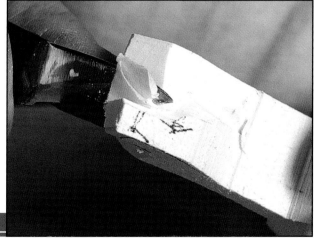

3

Trim away the wood from around and below the thumb, leaving it exposed. Notice the curve in the top of the thumb at the start of the thumbnail and the way the thumb is more slender behind the first knuckle.

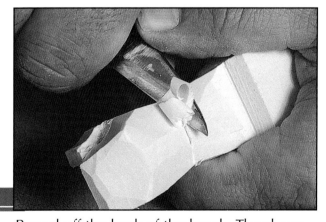

4

Round off the back of the hand. The shape of the hand is trapezoidal. The distance from the wrist to the knuckle of the index finger is about a third longer than the distance from the wrist to the knuckle of the little finger.

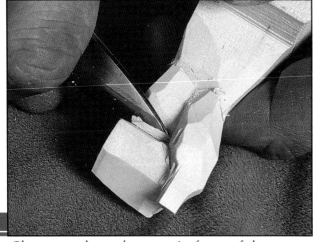

5 Clean out the palm area in front of the fingertips.

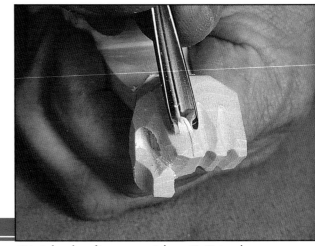

6 Divide the fingers with a "V" tool.

Carving an Open Hand

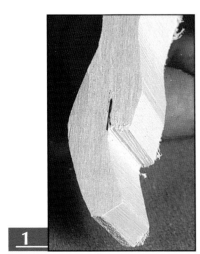

1 Using the pattern, cut out the open hand.

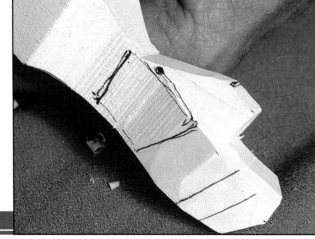

2 Outline the thumb with a V tool and trim away excess wood.

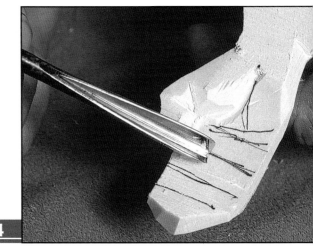

3 Define the shape of the back of the hand and the position of the knuckles.

4 Indicate the location of the opposite side o the knuckles where the hand will fold. These folds are known as lifelines. The fol of the fingers where they join the hand is midway between the first and second knuckles.

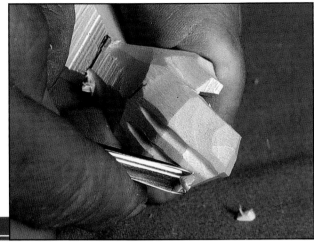

5 Define the fingers with a V tool.

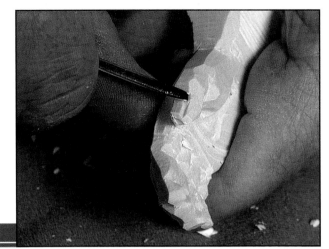

6 Detailing the thumb and fingers.

Take note:

The end of the thumb is just shy of the second knuckle of the index finger. The index and ring fingers are about the same length, except that the ring finger of the male is slightly longer and the index finger of the female is slightly longer. The little finger is about as long as the first knuckle of the ring finger. Usually I will carve the nail of the thumb, but not the fingers. It seems to me that the fingernails are too small to be of any value in a carving of this size. Therefore, the wrinkles at the back of the knuckles are also unnecessary and not even seen on the closed hand because the flesh of the fingers is stretched around the bone.

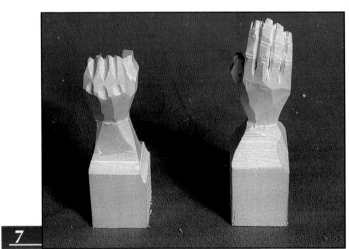

7 Back view of completed hands.

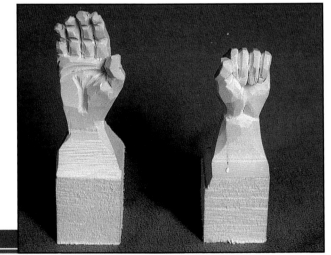

8 Palm view of completed hands.

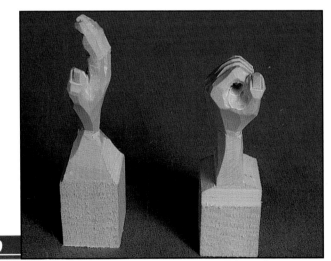

9 Thumb side view of completed hands.

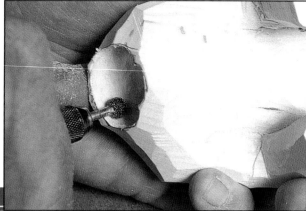

1

Before we start carving the clothing, attach the torso and the head. Prepare the torso to insert the head by carving an opening to accept the shape of the neck.

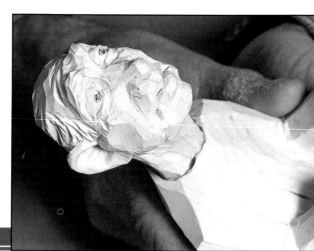

2

This photo shows the torso with the head inserted.

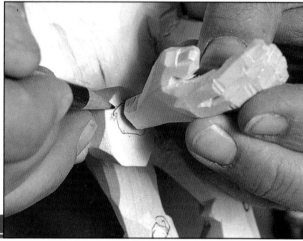

3

Use a pencil to outline the wrist so that the hole will be the correct size. Notice that the shape of the wrist is not round, but actually wider from thumb to little finger and narrow from front to back.

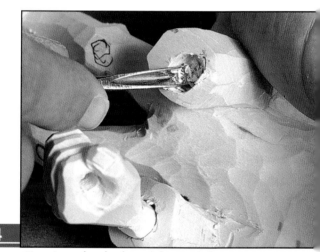

4

Carving the hole with a 3/8" gouge.

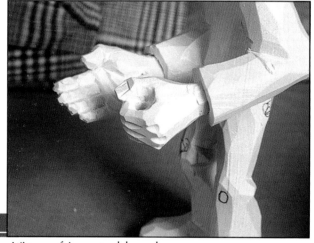

5

View of inserted hands.

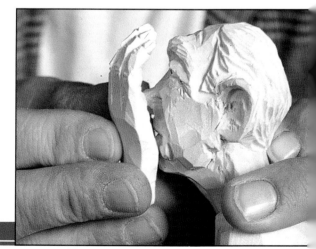

6

View of head and hand showing the comparative proportions of hands and face. Remember, the wrist to fingertip measurement will equal the chin to hairline measurement.

Carving

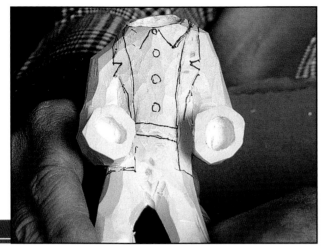

7 Draw in the clothing detail.

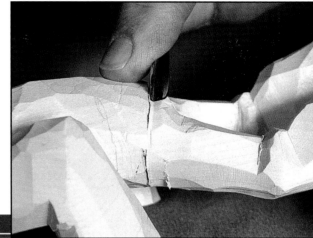

8 Outline the jacket with a V tool. The length of the jacket can vary by what appeals to you.

Take note:

It may help to get into the right frame of mind before laying out and carving the clothing. The material that makes up the clothing is basically flat and without form until we put a figure into it. Therefore we must consider the form of the underlying figure in each element of the clothing that we will be carving.

I find it easiest to consider the arms and legs as segmented cylinders. Where the cylinders meet at the elbows and knees, the shapes bend. These bent shapes cause stress on the fabric that covers the shapes. That stress causes the material to fold and drape.

Always consider the arm or leg under the material when laying out the folds so that you won't carve off the form that lies beneath. The shoulders will determine how the jacket will hang. The first folds that we will create are the larger, more prominent folds and drapes. These larger forms are what most carvers leave out of their carving.

The folds that are generally carved into the average figure are the wrinkle folds at the back of the knees and in front of the elbows. That's what our subconscious mind knows to be there, but many times they are actually less visible to the eye than those folds that are left off the figure. We allow our mind to kind of wipe out some of what we need to see. Again, it is important to see the subject and take time to notice what our eye is seeing, rather than what our mind is interpreting.

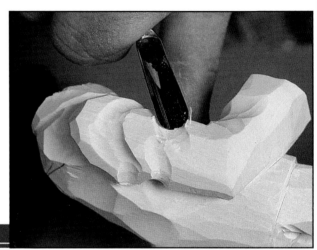

9 Lay in the folds and wrinkles of the jacket and pants with a large gouge. It is important to set up the major folds first so that the details will be shown on the form that's created. There is no interest when you have details on flat form.

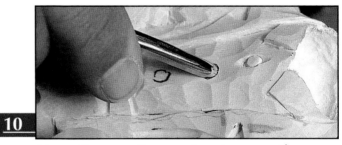

10 Use a 2mm or 3mm veiner to carve the buttons. Be sure to set the edge of the button with a stop cut angling away from the button so that the button won't pop off. Odd numbers create better visual interest than even numbers. Therefore we want to show three or five buttons rather than two or four.

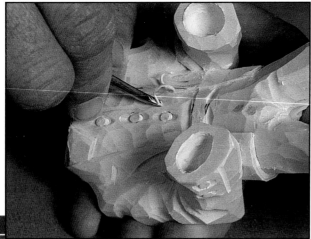

11

The buttons are carved before the edge of the shirt placard (the seams on both sides of the buttons) is carved. That will make it much easier to establish the necessary width to include the button. Carving the buttons after the placard is established makes it hard to keep the buttons inside the established limits and often results in breakout around the button.

13

Begin detailing the feet, the shoes and the pants.

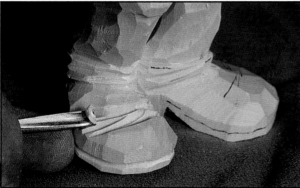

14

The shoe bends where the toes attach to the foot. Outline the sole of the shoe and carve some folds in the top of the shoe where it bends. Although we carve the folds with a V tool, the end result is a positive shape between the cuts indicating the leather of the shoe bunching up.

12

Set the heels of the shoes by first making a stop cut in front of the heel and carving away the bottom of the shoe sole to determine the thickness of the heel. This cut is generally against the grain of the wood so a slicing cut with a very sharp knife is necessary to keep the cut clean.

Take note:
As we get down to detailing the feet, the shoes and the pants where they come in contact with the feet, we want to be mindful of the muscle structure, most especially the calf muscle at the back of the leg. The pants will hang from this muscle and drape down towards the shoe then blouse up where they contact the shoe. The toe of the shoe always curves up so that it sits up above the floor. It matters not what type of footwear your figure is wearing; the toes always turn up. We also need to indicate the knob of the kneecap with a shallow gouge cut below the knee.

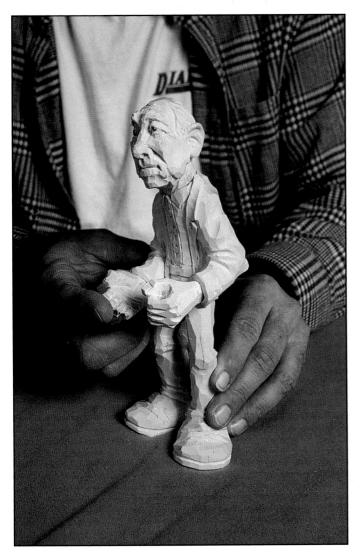

This photo shows the completed figure with head and hands attached.

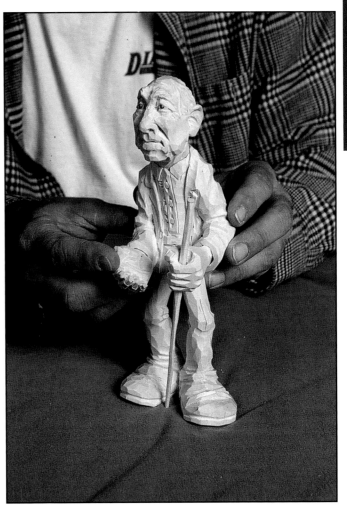

Here you see the completed figure with a staff inserted into the closed hand.

Chapter Six

Painting the Old Man

To color this figure, we are using acrylic paints that are thinned to a wash consistency that will impart color to the carving without obliterating the grain of the wood. The term "wash" is used to describe a transparent water based stain created by thinning or mixing water with your acrylic paints. I believe that there is nothing worse for a carving than to finish a piece in wood and then have it look like it may be ceramic, so the wood grain must show through.

End grain will absorb more than side grain and therefore will pull in more pigment making the end grain darker. To achieve a more even color, I first seal the wood by dunking the carving in water. This doesn't actually seal the carving, but makes the surface more consistent with regard to its ability to accept the wash evenly. The first color I use on my figure is a very light wash of burnt sienna. I cover the entire figure with this color before adding any other colors. This burnt sienna wash acts as a base coat that will actually subdue the tone of the other colors that are added on top of this color and will enhance the wood grain.

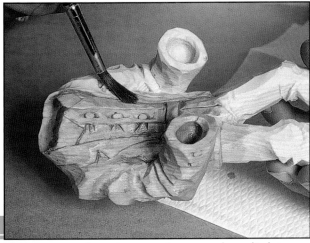

1 After preparing the carving, apply a light wash of burnt sienna to the body.

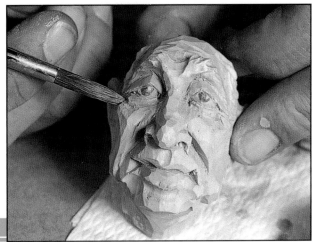

2 Next apply a light wash of medium flesh to all areas where the flesh is exposed. I then use a color called Caucasian Flesh in all areas where there would be shadows.

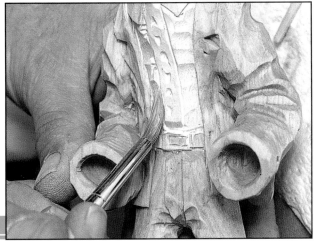

3 I use a dirty white color called sandstone for the shirt.

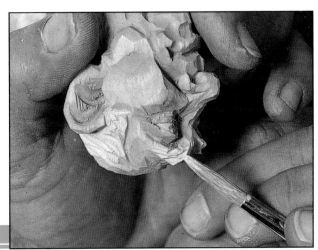

4 The same sandstone color on the shirt is used for a second base coat on the hair and eyebrows.

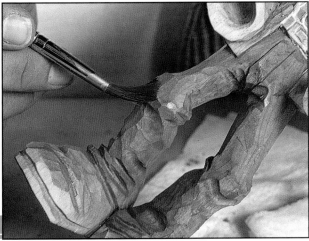

5 A second coat of burnt sienna is applied to the pants to intensify the base coat.

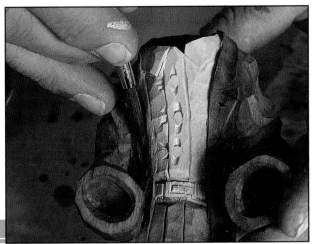

6 A mixture of charcoal and burnt umber is applied to the coat and shoes.

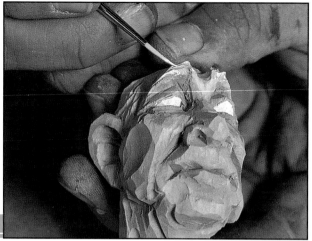

7

A coat of antique white is applied to the eyes.

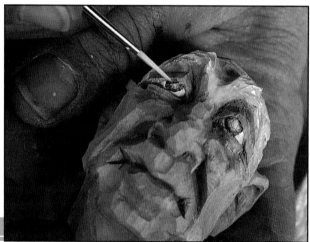

8

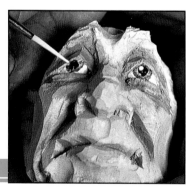

10

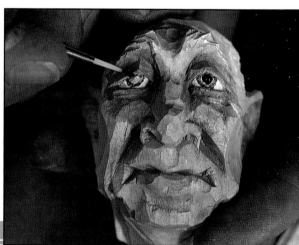

9

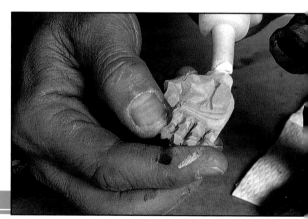

11

Take note:

To cover the eye and create an effective representation of the eyeball, I use the eye color pretty much straight from the bottle undiluted. The antique white is also dry brushed onto the eyebrows and hair to highlight the color. Dry brushing is, just as the term implies, simply dabbing your brush into the color and working most of the color out onto your pallet before applying the color to your carving. The brush is almost dry and the color goes only onto the high spots of your carving.

After the white of the eye is completely dry, you can apply the color of the iris. The outer edge of the iris is dark and fades to a softer, lighter color as it approaches the pupil. There are a variety of ways to accomplish this task, but the technique that works best for me is to wipe my brush clean after applying the color, and lift some of the color away from the center of the iris while the color is still wet.

To finish the eye, I apply a very small spot of antique white to the edge of the pupil indicating a reflection of light. This gives the eye a little sparkle and makes it come to life. Be sure to have the white highlight spot in the same location on each eye, usually at the intersection of the pupil and the iris.

The next step in painting the eye is to do the pupil. I use a color called charcoal for the pupil because I don't like using black or white in my pallet. Black is too stark and is the result of pigment reflecting no color. White is just the opposite, reflecting all colors of the spectrum. Both colors are unappealing and too stark for me.

It is now time to glue the head and hands to the figure. At this point you need to be sure that you are happy with the colors because this is the last chance you will have to make corrections.

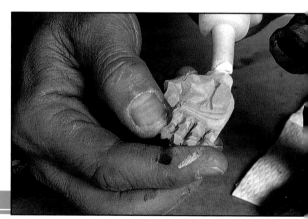

12

I now brush on a wax product to protect the carving. Apply the wax to the entire carving and let it sit for 30 minutes. Then wipe all excess wax from the carving and use a soft bristle brush to buff the wax to a nice luster.

Take note:
The wax that I use is produced by Watco and is their "natural color" finishing wax. This wax product is highly flammable and can and will spontaneously combust and cause a fire if the rags used to wipe and clean are left wadded up and not properly disposed of. Be sure to follow all precautions on the label.
CAUTION: If you haven't properly sealed your carving with this natural wax, the dark wax applied later during the antiquing stage will penetrate into the pores of the wood and ruin your carving.

13

Mix an antiquing medium using a combination of Watco natural wax and Watco dark wax. The ratio of this mixture is approximately 1 part dark wax to 5 parts natural.

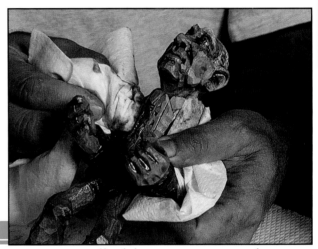

14

I now wipe all of the antiquing wax from the surface of the figure leaving it in the recesses to enhance the depth of the cuts.

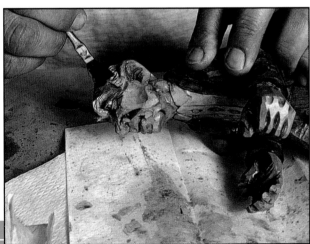

15

If the recesses are too dark, use a brush to lift some of the wax out. After lifting the excess wax with the brush, wipe your brush on a towel to clean before trying to lift more or you will just be moving the wax around to another area of the figure.

16

Rewipe the carving and allow the wax to completely dry before buffing with a soft bristle brush.

Caricature Carving from Head to Toe • 53

Painting

Chapter Seven

Three Additional Caricature Projects

The three carvings in this section of additional projects were chosen because I feel that they best represent the diversity of my work to this point in my carving career.

The baseball pitcher (see pages 57–60) is an old timer who still has the moves but has lost the physique. We have an Over 40 league in Phoenix, and I enjoy watching the guys who actually had a career in baseball at one time and now play just for the love of the game.

The cowboy with the bottle (see pages 61–64) is a carving that can hold any 50 mm size bottle including the sample sizes that are most often found on the airplanes. This guy has a bottle that has been labeled as "Cactus Jack's Snake Oil – Guaranteed – Worms yer' horse and makes ugly women attractive." Such an elixir would have been very desirable in the Old West.

The Santa (see pages 65–69) is an example of the "Old World Revival Style" that we find has become very popular with collectors. This fellow exhibits a pleasant smile and is holding a birdhouse in one hand for the cardinal in the opposite hand—sort of a big bird in the hand with a bush is worth more than a birdhouse that's too small (or something like that).

Carved by Dave Stetson;
painted by Michele Carville

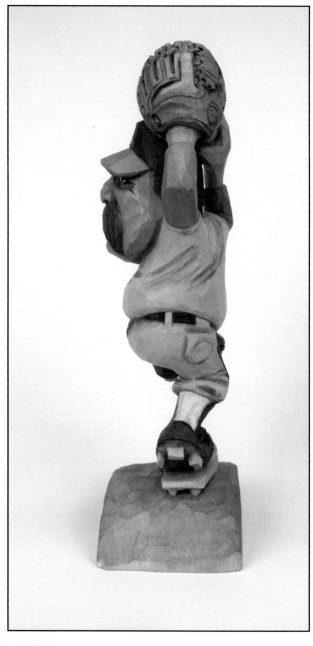

Carved by Dave Stetson;
painted by Michele Carville

Chapter Eight

Gallery

This gallery of carvings provides you with examples of my work to show what can be accomplished using the information provided in this book. Inspiration is something that we all need to be creative and it can be found in a variety of ways and places. I hope that you will find inspiration from the gallery and be encouraged to try some of these or something different for yourself.

The first figure that I carved holding a small whiskey bottle. The logistics of carving this piece involved creating a figure that would hold a bottle, thus sizing the figure to a bottle and having it balance. From this first carving I then created a master figure from which rough outs could be produced.

Back view showing how a broken fence added some visual interest to the base.

Front and back views of a bottle holding cowboy that was carved from a rough out. This figure is wearing a wide brim bolero style hat with a Sunday suit.

Typical moustache cowboy wearing a bib front shirt and neck scarf.

Another version of the bottle cowboy wearing a dust scarf with suspenders on his pants and rolled up shirt sleeves with his pants tucked into his boots.

Front view of the seated rifleman.

Back view of the seated rifleman.

Old timer baseball pitcher was inspired by some of the over forty league pitchers that I've seen. They still have all the moves of their younger days, but the physique has changed.

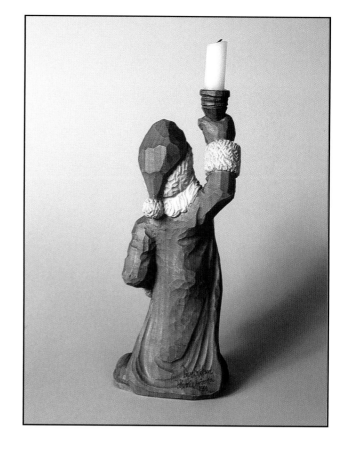

Santa holding a candle is a project that I designed for a class that wanted something different in an heirloom Santa. Designing it was real easy because I don't know what an "heirloom" Santa is supposed to look like, so anything that I created would be different.

Small sheriff figure that was designed to show action and movement is the subject of this carving. The figure is turning to his right and looking back to his left.

Same sheriff pose with a slightly different hat and wearing a woodcarver's name tag instead of a badge.

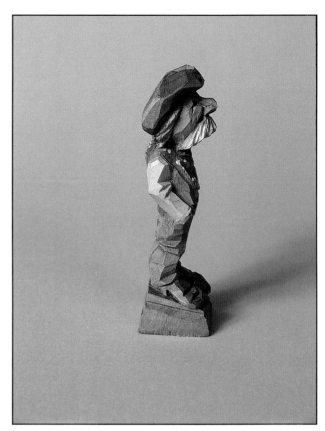

Carving of a Little Hombre done from a five-step casting that shows how to carve this figure in the round.

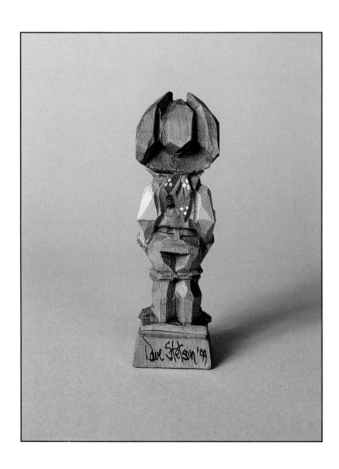

Series of small male head studies.

Cowboy shooting a hole in his boot and showing a pained expression.

Series of small female head studies.

Pair of rabbit bottle stoppers.

More head studies.

Cowboy bust.

Series of head studies.

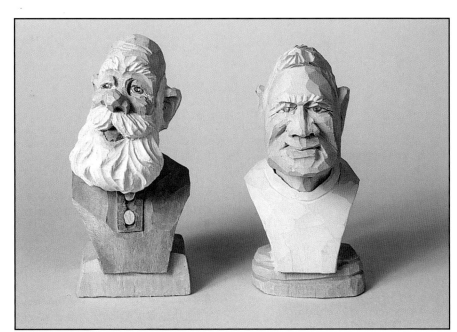

Santa head and male bust.

Series of head studies.

Three more views of the core project in this book.

Four figures of elderly gentlemen. These figures were designed to show what can be accomplished from studying this book.

Standing figure of cowboy with moustache.

Cowboy golfer.

 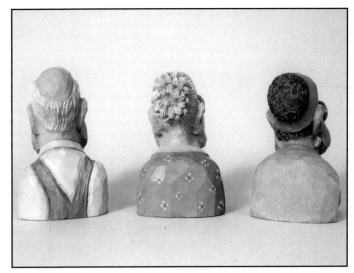

Front and back views of a small bust. All three busts were carved from the same pattern.

Cowboy busts carved from the same pattern.

Busts wearing baseball caps carved from the same pattern.

Series of cowboy busts carved from the same pattern.

Front and side views of a pair of female busts.

Mountain man bust with a live coonskin cap.

Pair of Vikings with different expressions.

Sea captain at the helm. Figure designed to show the coat blowing and captain holding his hat in the wind.

Happy Santa with cardinal on top of his staff.

Cowboy Santa with a stick horse.

Santa with a staff.

Simple stick Santa with carved rocking horse.

Santa designed by Nancy Goff, carved by Dave Stetson and painted by Michele Carville.

Santa with emphasis on creating a kindly face.

Santa with bag of gifts that was inspired by a Russian carving.

White Santa holding carved lantern with candle.

(The santas on these two pages were carved by Dave Stetson and painted by Michele Carville.)

Carving of a dancing fiddler, unpainted. With this particular figure I have his long moustache caught up in the strings of his bow and fiddle.

These photos are of a series of flat back heads that could be used as bola ties, pins or refrigerator magnets.

Carving of an old man putting on his socks in the morning.

Notes:

More Great Project Books from Fox Chapel Publishing

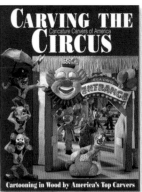

Carving the Caricature Carvers of America Circus
Cartooning in Wood by America's Top Carvers
By Caricature Carvers of America

Over 30 patterns from a balancing act to a zany zebra along with expert tips from top carvers.

ISBN: 978-1-56523-094-1
$19.95 · 128 Pages

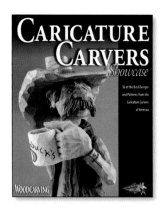

Caricature Carvers Showcase
50 of the Best Designs and Patterns from the Caricature Carvers of America
By Caricature Carvers of America

Learn to carve whimsical caricatures with 50 original patterns, carving techniques, and painting tips from The Caricature Carvers of America.

ISBN: 978-1-56523-337-9
$19.95 · 128 Pages

Carving the Full Moon Saloon
The Art of Caricature in Wood
By Caricature Carvers of America

Saddle up with more than 25 patterns of western folks & their friends, including expert tips from top carvers.

ISBN: 978-1-56523-056-9
$19.95 · 128 Pages

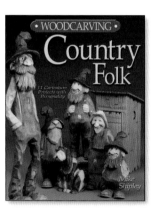

Woodcarving Country Folk
11 Caricature Projects with Personality
By Mike Shipley

Develop your caricature carvings skills with expert step-by-step instructions for 12 whimsical caricature projects with personality.

ISBN: 978-1-56523-286-0
$14.95 · 88 Pages

Santa Showcase
Celebrate the Season with 24 Patterns from the Best of Woodcarving Illustrated
By editors of *Woodcarving Illustrated*

The best and most-popular Santa projects from the past 10 years of *Woodcarving Illustrated*, these 20 patterns and four step-by-step projects represent the craftsmanship and good cheer of carving's top artists.

ISBN 978-1-56523-340-9
$16.95 · 96 Pages

Carving Fantasy & Legend Figures in Wood
Patterns & Instructions for Dragons, Wizards & Other Creatures of Myth
By Shawn Cipa

Step-by-step projects and 12 patterns for popular mythical creatures, including a wizard, unicorn, troll, gargoyle, phoenix and gryphon from the legendary carver, Shawn Cipa.

ISBN: 978-1-56523-254-9
$17.95 · 120 Pages

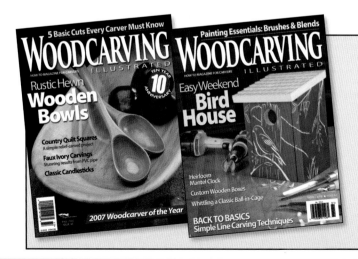

WOODCARVING
ILLUSTRATED

In addition to being a leading source of woodworking books and DVDs, Fox Chapel also publishes Woodcarving Illustrated. Released quarterly, it delivers premium projects, expert tips and techniques from today's finest carvers, and in-depth information about the latest tools, equipment, & materials.

Subscribe Today!
Woodcarving Illustrated: **888-506-6630**
www.WoodcarvingIllustrated.com